VIOLENCE IN THE ARTS

VIOLENCE IN
THE ARTS

JOHN FRASER

CAMBRIDGE UNIVERSITY PRESS

Published by the Syndics of the Cambridge University Press
Bentley House, 200 Euston Road, London NW1 2DB
American Branch: 32 East 57th Street, New York, N.Y. 10022

© Cambridge University Press 1974

Library of Congress Catalogue Card Number: 73-84319

ISBN: 0 521 20331 7

First published 1974
Second printing 1974

Printed in the United States of America

TO CAROL
without whom, nothing

CONTENTS

PREFACE

This book is a personal essay, not a survey or a piece of sociology. I am primarily concerned with some of the ways in which, to borrow from D. H. Lawrence, 'our sympathies flow and recoil' in our dealings with violence in the arts, and with why it is that some violences seem to make for intellectual clarity and a more civilized consciousness, while others make for confusion. In the first three chapters I look at various problems involved in trying to think clearly about the subject, and at certain over-simple ways of coping with them. In chapters 4 and 5, which are the heart of the book, I attempt to work out an informal poetics with respect to the victims and the perpetrators of violences. In the final three chapters I am concerned with the question of violence and thought, and attempt to move beyond the positions sketched in the first three, particularly where 'protest' art is concerned.

Since my topic is large and I am chiefly interested in principles, I have not tried to be comprehensive in my choice of examples, and each reader will no doubt think of obvious ones that I have failed to give. Contrariwise, when I offer some of my extended lists of titles, I am not assuming that all the works will be familiar to everyone. I have taken a good many of my examples from movies, since these days movies are what classical Latin literature once was to educated people – the one cultural topic that they almost all have in common and feel strongly about.

I have also drawn a number from thrillers of various kinds, of which I have read a lot and which are sometimes usefully paradigmatic.

In places, too, I touch on non-fictional violences. Not only does the formal gap between fiction and non-fiction disappear at times, in the sense that there can sometimes be no way of telling whether a particular stretch of grainy film, taken out of its context, comes from a documentary using Nouvelle Vague techniques or from a work of fiction imitating documentary techniques; or whether a stretch of narrative, taken out of context, comes from a work of autobiography, or history, or anthropology, or from a novel; or whether a particular stretch in a novel (e.g., *Moby Dick*) is invented, or is derived from someone else's account, or is a literal record of what the writer himself witnessed. Beyond this is the fact that the great majority of us, when we speak of actual violences, are still speaking primarily of passages that we have read, or things that people have said to us, or images that we have seen on television or in the cinema. And even when certain violences, such as those of Nazism, exist in our minds as a composite image, that image still usually has a kind of form to it, a structure of settings and characters, that in some ways resembles that of a long novel, or a very long documentary programme, or a work of history with some of the densities and resonances of art.

I have cut across genres very freely, and have juxtaposed works of widely varying merits without continually indicating that I recognize the differences between them. I am aware, however, that a term like The Western covers a wide variety of works, none of which is as distinguished as a number of non-Westerns, such as Pabst's *Lulu*, or Vigo's *L'Atalante*, or Eisenstein's *Strike*, or Resnais' *Nuit et brouillard*, or Mizoguchi's *Ugetsu*

Monagatari, or Renoir's *Partie de campagne,* or Buñuel's *L'Age d'Or;* and I believe that in the end the essential critical task is discrimination, even though this cannot be done effectively without an intelligent awareness of genres, forms, and conventions.[1] I have not involved myself with the question of censorship except parenthetically, since to have done so at the necessary length would have taken me too far from my main argument. But my attitude will probably be plain enough, and I have gone into the subject elsewhere.[2]

As to procedures, I have not provided bibliographical information about novels, short stories, and the like, except when quoting from a translation, or about non-fictional works that are available in several places, such as George Orwell's 'Raffles and Miss Blandish'. For the most part my quotations from foreign-language works are taken from translations, though occasionally, when the original was particularly rich in some way, I have quoted from it and put a translation in the notes. Occasionally, too, I have provided my own translation of a passage. Throughout, in an attempt to lessen confusion, I have referred to movie directors by their last names only, and to other creators by their full names except when to do so would have been pedantic.

I would like to express my gratitude to the following: to my father, Ivan Kenneth Fraser, whose influence, though he may not recognize it, is present in many of these pages; to Thomas J. Roberts, from whom I never cease to learn; to Yvonne Waage, for over twenty years of indispensable friendship and encouragement; to Richard Cody, who knows his Orwell and will understand what I am talking about; and to Michael Black, who found the right words to say and got me to write this book. My heaviest debt is to my wife, to whom this book is dedicated. The book is based on three articles that appeared in the *Partisan Review*, the *Western Humanities Review*, and the *Southern Review*. I would like to thank the editors of those journals for permission to use material that first appeared in their pages.

JOHN FRASER

1

INTRODUCTORY

In retrospect, one of the most symbolic cultural events of the 1960s was the appearance of Susan Sontag's 'Notes on "Camp"' in the *Partisan Review*.[1] On the face of things, it was incongruous that this apologia for 'the sensibility of failed seriousness, of the theatricalization of experience', should have appeared in that particular journal. It was a sort of *Putsch* by the attitudes of the sophisticated queer underground, an aggressive parade under a respectable sponsor (Sontag playing Ludendorff) of the kinds of febrile witty sillinesses previously only observable in strength at campy parties; it created an influential axis with Marshall McLuhan's *Understanding Media*, which appeared in the same year (1964); and it assisted the various anti-critical forces at work inside the academy in traditional disciplines like English. Yet it was appropriate all the same that the article should have appeared in the quarterly that had stood so much for earnestness of thought, a resolute probing of the anxieties and ills of the *Zeitgeist*, an anti-formalist critical approach, and a general committedness of a sort that had made it seem eminently natural in the 1940s for someone like George Orwell to appear in its pages. The Camp attitudes – and campiness had been around for years before Sontag enabled it to come out into the streets – are only an intensification of tendencies towards evasion in all of us, and the evident thankfulness with which the idea of Camp was received on both sides of the Atlantic testified to how strong the strains had become in a certain kind of intellectual strenuousness.

It was in sexual matters, of course, that intellectual collapses and restructurings were most apparent during the 1960s. 'Notes on "Camp"', for instance, was as much about sexual styles as it was about aesthetic ones, and it obviously contributed to the recognition of a considerably wider range of sexual behaviour than hitherto; a recognition, I mean, not merely of physical activities in the Kinsey fashion but of activities involving the whole personality in cultural relationships. But violence too seems to me to have been, in one way and another, a considerable area of strain, not least because so much of the lowbrow fare that had given so many intellectuals so much pleasure in their youth – gangster movies, radio serials, comic books, and so on – had involved violence. What interests me in this chapter is the way in which the 1960s witnessed not only an intensification of the violences in violent works, but a change in the attitudes of intellectuals towards them that paralleled to some extent the sexual shift. There was not, it seems to me, a proportionate increase in intellectual clarity, for understandable reasons. Respectable theorizing in English about the vagaries of sex goes back at least to Havelock Ellis and Edward Carpenter, and creative explorations of them to Lawrence and Joyce, and the literature on the subject is by now immense. Violence, on the other hand, is even now something of a terra incognita intellectually. 'No one engaged in thought about history and politics,' observed Hannah Arendt in *On Violence* at the end of the 1960s, 'can remain unaware of the enormous role violence has always played in human affairs, and it is at first glance rather surprising that violence has been singled out so seldom for special consideration. (In the last edition of the Encyclopedia of the Social Sciences "violence" does

2

not even rate an entry.)'[2] Hence the changes in America where art was concerned were peculiarly problematic.

What took place was a striking shift away from the attitude that Robert Warshow had described in 1954 when he remarked that:

> One of the well-known peculiarities of modern civilized opinion is its refusal to acknowledge the value of violence. . . . We train ourselves to be shocked or bored by cultural images of violence, and our very concept of heroism tends to be a passive one. . . . In art, though we may still be able to understand and participate in the values of the Iliad, a modern writer like Ernest Hemingway we find somewhat embarrassing: there is no doubt that he stirs us, but we cannot help recognizing also that he is a little childish. And in the criticism of popular culture . . . the presence of images of violence is often assumed to be in itself a sufficient ground for condemnation.[3]

And entailed in that shift was an abandonment of the ground rules that had been laid down for American liberals in G. Legman's *Love and Death* (1949) and Fredric Wertham's *Seduction of the Innocent* (1954)[4] and that ultimately derived from Orwell's classic analysis of James Hadley Chase's *No Orchids for Miss Blandish* in 1944. 'The interconnection between sadism, masochism, success worship, power worship, nationalism and totalitarianism,' Orwell had pointed out, 'is a huge subject whose edges have barely been scratched, and even to mention it is considered somewhat indelicate.'[5] He himself had drawn attention to some of those interconnections in Chase's thriller, and Wertham and Legman had followed him where the social attitudes implicit in the bloodier comic books and in more respectable works of entertainment were concerned.[6]

It is clear why attacks like Wertham's and Legman's should have carried the emotional charge and exerted the influence that they did. The late 1940s and early 1950s in America were not only years of psychic recuperation from one war and reluctant involvement in another. They were also the McCarran–McCarthy years, a period during which the confrontation between liberal intellectualism and its opposite reached a peculiarly dramatic intensity, with the amount of power at stake greater than before. And in this context the political implications of certain works when read in a more or less Orwellian fashion were inescapable, above all those of Micky Spillane, the most violent thriller writer thitherto outside of the underground pulps of the 1930s.[7] It was a shock to observe the total commitment with which an author selling in the hundreds of thousands was attacking so many of the accepted social crime-fictional decencies, such as publicly administered justice, the rights of criminals or suspected criminals as citizens, the need to keep private investigation in line with official procedures (unless, as in Dashiell Hammett and Raymond Chandler, law officers were patently corrupt, in which case the private investigator was simply acting as a *de facto* lawman himself), and the acknowledgment of a reasonably wide range of motives and dispositions among criminals and of proportionate degrees of punishment. This was the voice of the punitive American Right in full cry; and similarly antiliberal attitudes, even if sometimes skilfully camouflaged, were discernible in a disconcerting number of other popular works.

But Joe McCarthy, the archetypal Bad Guy, was stopped at last, if not by the Good Sheriff, at least by the Decent Townspeople, which was perhaps even more reassuring. And when subsequently John Kennedy took over the presidency it began to look as if the long-standing contest between high-souled intellectual liberalism and a menacing know-nothing illiberalism was effectively finished where national power was concerned, and as if America were at last going to enter into something like the political civility that Britain had enjoyed for so many decades. The result was a sudden lowering of tensions and increase of expectations that manifested itself alike in the image-makers' unprecedented concern with 'style', the intensified formalism of the visual arts, and the general sense among intellectuals that a little friskiness might now be permissible. And this depoliticizing of certain areas, this feeling that there might now be room for the merely aesthetic, had its effects on people's reactions to violent works. I can still recall picking up in the later 1950s an ill-printed paperback with an ugly cover called *Casino Royale*, by an author whom I had never heard of, and standing beside the drug-store book-rack and reading a far more disgusting account of a torturing than the one in *No Orchids*, and hoping that no one I knew would come in and catch me. And I can also recall writing a few years later a critical article on Pauline Réage's *Story of O*, and feeling that I was putting myself at risk by treating it respectfully, and being quite certain that *this* book, at any rate, would never appear outside France. But as everyone knows, no less a liberal eminence than President Kennedy himself announced that he was a fan of Ian Fleming's books, with gratifying effects on their sales.[8] And then the Bond movies clinched matters by making nasty violences *fun*, in a rather campy way, just as Terry Southern and Mason Hoffenberg's *Candy* made certain hitherto taboo kinds of eroticism fun and very campy indeed. Among the results was that when sexual censorship really started collapsing, it became possible for a good many works that were both erotic *and* violent, such as *Story of O*, William Burroughs' *Naked Lunch*, and a lot of the less prestigious books put out by the Olympia Press and the Grove Press, to be granted an unprecedented kind of respectability. They too were officially 'entertaining' now; they too were in some degree Camp, along with a number of things that some of us had uncampily enjoyed long before Sontag's 'Notes' appeared. And, given the further liberalizations since, and the plethora of more or less sado-masochistic erotica now available on respectable drug-store book-racks, the kind of embarrassment that I testified to above begins to look as quaint as the hula-hoop.

The general raising of the shock threshold during the past decade has probably been especially welcome for members of the movie-going generation that came to consciousness in the 1930s, a generation entranced by the great compelling images of terror and violence in the thrillers and horror movies of that period, and knowing intimately what T. S. Eliot was talking about when he said:

> Those who have lived before such terms as 'high-brow fiction', 'thrillers' and 'detective fiction' were invented realize that melodrama is perennial and that the craving for it is perennial and must be satisfied. If we cannot get this satisfaction out of what the publishers present as 'literature', then we will read – with less and less pretence of concealment – what we call 'thrillers'.[9]

It can still be an immense pleasure to relax and satisfy a yearning for darkness and terror ('the backward half-look/Over the shoulder, towards the primitive terror') in a world of mysteries where, as in the Hall of Heorot invaded by Grendel, hairy monstrous hands come out of panels over beds, and indescribable Things drive men mad with terror at mere glimpses of them. And a good many of us, I assume, understand too what Lee Marvin was talking about when he remarked, apropos of Siegel's *The Killers*:

> In the opening, me and my partner sidle into a blind home looking for a doublecrosser. I get behind the head blind dame, grab her by the throat and push her almost to the floor. 'Where's Johnny North?' I breathe in her ear. So she tells us. I barge into the room knocking the blindees over – we used real ones – and I say 'You Johnny North?' He says yeah. So we take out our guns and we put ten bullets in him straight up and down his middle. It's great. And everybody out front is getting their vicaries [vy-*care*-ease; vicarious thrills].[10]

Most of us have got our 'vicaries' from time to time from works that we have known to be defective in all kinds of ways, but which are informed by a combination of gusto and ruthlessness that leaves one feeling simultaneously relaxed and toned up, the supreme example probably being the glorious thirty-two volume series of Pierre Souvestre and Marcel Allain in 1910–14, beloved of the Surrealists, in which Chief Inspector Jouve of the Sûreté and his assistant the journalist Fandor pursue the quintessential master-criminal Fantomas through a *Faerie-Queene*-like labyrinth of disguisings and unmaskings, atrocities foiled and greater atrocities accomplished, with a cast of thousands, some scenes of a stunning poetic force, and a probably unequalled presentation of Paris *apaches* and their argot. More insidiously, it can even be a pleasure to give way at times to the feeling expressed in the great French actress Réjane's 'J'ai besoin de m'encanailler un peu' ('I need a bit of low-life')[11] and to allow oneself to enjoy something precisely because it *is* terrible as art – and the more terrible the better; pleasurable, that is, to surrender oneself temporarily to works that outrage one's conscious critical standards because they are muddled or stupid or nasty. So it is easy enough to see why the notions of Camp and the related Pop should have been so welcomed. They gave intellectuals, especially academics, a respectable pretext for continuing to indulge in, or for returning to, certain real and private pleasures without having to feel any longer that they were thereby demonstrating an incorrigible badness of taste and betraying their professional standards irredeemably.

In some ways, moreover, it is a good thing critically that the power of various works to shock has been diminishing, insofar as that entails getting away from a too narrowly mimetic response to them. Only in terms of such a response can one explain the discrepancies between most of the indignant descriptions of particular fictional horrors given by Legman and the jejuneness of the episodes themselves, or the kinds of commendations by reviewers ('spine-chilling', 'a nightmare of suspense', and so on) that one encounters on the dust-jackets of thrillers of unrelieved flatness and banality. And a fair amount of the discussion about censorship and about the possible harm done to the young by works of violence has obviously been bedevilled by excessive responsiveness to plot and insufficient alertness to the range and variety of conventions that are often involved. As the researches of psychologists like Hilde Himmelweit and her associates indicate[12] (and as Saturday afternoon cinema-going tends to confirm), the young may in some ways be more accurate than some of their elders in their perceptions of a good deal of fictional violence, and better able to distinguish between realistic and stylized

8

violences, intentionally and unintentionally comic ones, and so on, than is often allowed for. Moreover, even a little reflection about one's own viewing and reading can remind one of the multifariousness of the term 'violence in art', and the variety of responses that may be called for at different times.

There is in fact no one thing, no chemically insolatable and analysable substance, that is violence, any more than there is one thing that is sex, even though it is easy to slip into talking as if there were. As Hans Toch observes in *Violent Men*, 'the concern with violence is directed at a myth. It demands an ocean where there are islands; it constructs a monolith in place of diversity; it calls for formulas to cover complexity; and it presumes cure-alls where we have no diagnosis.'[18] The range of actual violences is enormous – vastly greater than that of sex – including, as they do, love bites and the assassination of Caesar, African safaris and the vivisectional activities of Claude Bernard, football matches and the flogging-blocks at Dachau, the battle of Britain and the guillotining of Landru, and so on. The functions of violence are also numerous – violence as release, violence as communication, violence as play, violence as self-affirmation, or self-defence, or self-discovery, or self-destruction, violence as a flight from reality, violence as the truest sanity in a particular situation, and so on. And just as the term 'erotic literature' logically covers works as various as *Antony and Cleopatra*, *The Miller's Tale*, *Les cent vingt jours de Sodome*, *Pamela*, *The Awkward Age*, and *Naked Lunch*, so a term like 'violence in literature' applies to works as various as *The Wind in the Willows*, *Moby Dick*, *I the Jury*, *Hamlet*, the *Grettir Saga*, *The Faerie Queene*, *Hansel and Gretel*, *The Mikado*, *In the Penal Colony*, *Oliver Twist*, *Phèdre*, *Histoire d'O*, *The March Up Country*, and the Book of Genesis.

9

Furthermore, the kinds of yearnings and fears that get catered to or played upon in works involving violence are obviously far more various than those that Maurice Edgar Coindreau pointed to when he observed that the distrust felt for the Grand Guignol theatre resulted substantially from 'the fact that the whole genre is addressed to instincts that people don't like to gratify except with the help of ingenious disguises and a rather childish hypocrisy. These instincts, which are the most deeply rooted in the human psyche, are, on the one hand, fear, on the other, the taste for blood and death.'[14]

For example: there is the yearning for totally untrammelled power and self-assertion (e.g., Alfred Jarry's *Ubu Roi*, Sade's *Juliette*, Marlowe's *Tamburlaine*). There is the yearning to be completely self-possessed and coolly manipulative in extreme situations (e.g., Dashiell Hammett's *Red Harvest*). There is the yearning to disrupt pretensions and decorums (e.g., Vigo's *Zéro de conduite*, the Marx Brothers' *A Night at the Opera*, Chaplin's *The Cure*) and also the fear of doing so (e.g., Clair's *The Italian Straw Hat*). There is the fear of becoming overwhelmed by internal psychic forces (e.g., the Jekyll and Hyde story) and the fear of being hopelessly corrupted by outside ones (e.g., the Dracula story). There are the mingled yearnings and fears epitomized in the Frankenstein story. There is the fear of being implacably hunted (e.g., William Godwin's *Caleb Williams*, Geoffrey Household's *Rogue Male*, Schoedsack and Pichel's *The Most Dangerous Game*) and the fear of entrapment in a group or institution containing hidden menaces (e.g., Leni's *The Cat and the Canary*, Whale's *The Old Dark House*). There is the yearning to prove oneself in a supreme test (e.g., Zinneman's *High Noon*, Stephen Crane's *The Red Badge of Courage*). There is the yearning to administer private justice with complete ruthlessness (e.g., Mickey

Spillane's *I The Jury*, Lang's *The Big Heat*, Kobayashi's *Harakiri*). There is the yearning to possess extraordinary physical skills (earned ones in Peter O'Donnell's *Modesty Blaise*, unearned ones in *Superman*) and the counter-poising yearning to be a bungler and yet have all one's errors turn out well (e.g., Keaton's *The General*). And there are a good many others, among them – as several of the works that I have mentioned demonstrate – the yearning to comport oneself with decency and dignity while engaging in violences, or, if losing control of one-self, to be brought back in the end to decency and dignity either by one's better self or by the intervention of people whom one respects. Furthermore, there is no necessary correlation between the ostensible seriousness or other-wise of a work, in terms of plot, and its actual merits. Aldrich, for instance, made what appears to have been a very distinguished movie out of Spillane's *Kiss Me Deadly*, and Franju's horror movie *Les yeux sans visage* ('adversely criticized in just about every country it played', according to Carlos Clarens in his *Illustrated History of the Horror Film*)[15] is one of the masterpieces of French cinema, just as Household's *Rogue Male* is one of the few decent British novels of the 1930s.

Nevertheless, there are obviously problems when one tries thinking seriously about the general thaw. On the one hand, it is agreeable to see the censors defeated and to be able to read works like Apollinaire's *Les onze mille verges* or Sade's *Juliette* without having to liberate them from some library *enfer*; or to see Grand Guignolesque movies like Lewis's *Blood Feast* if one feels like it; or to be able to look at some of those 'unspeakably filthy' graphics, violent or otherwise, that one used to come across titillating references to in one's impressionable adolescence. On the other hand, when one finds oneself reading a respectable British thriller in which among other things (*a*) a woman's head is slowly crushed between the gigantic hands of an acromegalic hoodlum, (*b*) a hoodlum is killed by the hero by having a grease gun stuffed down his throat and pumped, (*c*) a man's lips are *stapled* together to gag him (with a detailed account of the hero's subsequently cutting and prying the staples out of the swollen flesh without any anaesthetic), and (*d*) the master criminal is finally tied down over an enormous floodlight by the hero and left to broil to death[16] – well, one is liable to feel that something has been slipping a bit somewhere, in popular literature, or in oneself, or in both, as one also does when reading the description of the beating-up in Mario Puzo's *The Godfather* or the torture scene in Frederick Forsyth's *The Day of the Jackal*. And where serious works are concerned, there are passages enough in ones like Hubert Selby, Jr's *The Room* that must have left a good many readers in a similar state of uneasiness as to what was happening to them as they read them. It is true that we have literary theorists like Northrop Frye to reassure us that it is not what goeth into a man but what cometh out of him that defileth, and that nothing need be a bother if you approach it in a sufficiently detached and formalistic way. And Frye's colleague McLuhan has much enlarged people's repertoire of stratagems for avoiding coming sharply to judgment on anything. It seems to me, however, that even though for most of us it is probably impossible now to respond to certain badnesses with the unforced and unequivocal firmness or Orwell on *No Orchids* ('Now for a header into the cesspool'), that isn't a reason for self-congratulation.

What is more to the point is that for most of us a formalist detachment is in fact not possible where violence is concerned and that, willy-nilly, emotions are involved, especially in view of the repoliticizing of everything in the later 1960s. I shall postpone until the third chapter a consideration of the way in which radicalism tried to restore to certain kinds of violent works the charge of feeling and meaning that the Camp approach had been draining off. First, I wish to look more closely at certain kinds of ambivalences in people's reactions to violence.

AMBIVALENCES

A convenient starting point is the paradox that it is Kubrick's *A Clockwork Orange* rather than Coppola's *The Godfather* that has done the most to set off complaints in the early 1970s about excessive violence in movies.

In *A Clockwork Orange* there is only one killing (the battered corpse of the murdered woman not being shown to us), and virtually the only blood that we see, apart from a brief excerpt or two from a psychologically-devised 'therapeutic' movie, comes from the protagonist's own nose. In *The Godfather*, in contrast, we are shown with some vividness the following: a man garrotted after having his hand pinned to a bar-counter with a switch-blade knife; a man blown apart by four or five sub-machine guns at close range; two men shotgunned in an elevator; two men shot at table by their dining companion; a man on a massage-table shot through the eye; two men shot down while leaving church; a man shot while trapped in a revolving door; a man garrotted in a car; probably two or three other killings that I have forgotten; plus an attempted killing (five bullets in the body), a vicious street fight, and a man waking up in the morning to find that he is sharing his bed with the freshly severed head of his prize racehorse. Yet in the reviewers' accounts that I myself had come across before going to see them, it was *A Clockwork Orange* that was the horror show; *The Godfather*, in contrast, had sounded so much like family entertainment that I almost didn't go to see it at all. And it seems to me that an important reason for this general paradox was that the first – and to a lesser extent Peckinpah's *Straw Dogs*, which was inevitably associated with it – had touched upon ambiguities and ambivalences of feeling that the second had not.

To be sure, there are ambiguities enough where gangster movies like *The Godfather* are concerned. Commenting on an off-Broadway production in the late 1960s of *The Resistible Rise of Arturo Ui*, Brecht's gangster-story allegory of Hitler's climb to power, a *Time* magazine reviewer complained that 'in the U.S., the play takes on the eerie quality of a faintly sinister success story, in which an immigrant boy from Brooklyn overcomes his bad accent and deplorable manners to achieve dominion and power over the second largest city in the nation'.[1] And in view of the increasingly ominous growth and power of organized crime, the tradition of media sentimentality towards gangsters may be a luxury that it might be well to try to do without, at least in some of its manifestations. When *Life* magazine ran a masterly and infuriating analysis by James Mills a few years ago of the course of events in a then-recent trial of East Coast *mafiosi*,[2] it was disconcerting to find, while reading it, that the photographs were working insidiously but powerfully against the text and against all the reactions of one's consciously judging mind. The principal figure on trial had the coarse good looks, vitality, self-assurance, and specious charm of innumerable gangster-movie heroes. The intelligent, dedicated, persistent, and clearly extremely decent prosecuting attorney, on the other hand, looked all too much like the rather square kind of White Anglo-Saxon Protestant who has stood humourlessly for a jejune kind of law-and-orderliness in a good many movies. And the sum of the visual message was that not only had the final outcome of 'Not Guilty' been inevitable but that in terms of relative vitalities, collective as well as individual, it was somehow or other a just one as well. Such a reaction, if widely shared, is presumably symptomatic of the American ambivalence towards law and order, the general desire for order and resentment of laws; and it no doubt contributes to making a lawful order harder to achieve.

Nevertheless, it is perfectly understandable that the critical reception of *The Godfather* was as tolerant as it was, quite apart from the gusto and craftsmanship that went into the making of it, the agreeable *kitsch* elements provided by Brando's presence, and the *roman à clef* allusions. If many of us have always relished the classic American gangster movies, and if, as Hawks' *Scarface* demonstrated, one can hardly have too much gunplay in them, this is not simply because of a lust for blood and corpses. As the same reviewer for *Time* commented, 'Americans tend to regard gangsters with nostalgic indulgence as individualistic resistance fighters against society (witness the vast popularity of *Bonnie and Clyde*)', and Robert Warshow's analysis of the genre, 'The Gangster as Tragic Hero', is deservedly still a classic, despite the subsequent complicatings of the genre that Lawrence Alloway has drawn attention to in *Violent America*. In other words, *The Godfather* may have been morally ambiguous, but for the most part it was a thoroughly familiar, an almost *respectable* ambiguousness.

The same could not be said for *A Clockwork Orange*. The ambiguities in it, while familiar in a certain sense, are far from respectable. Though the actual rape episode in it occupies probably less than ten minutes, *A Clockwork Orange*, in its general resonances, is a particularly striking example of a genre which has not, so far as I know, been given a name, but which deserves one and which I shall call the Violation Movie. It belongs, as does *Straw Dogs*, with movies like Wyler's *The Desperate Hours*, Grauman's *Lady in a Cage*, Young's *Wait Until Dark*, Brooks' *In Cold Blood* and, to judge from an account of it in *Films and Filming*, Kazan's *The Visitors*, in which the principal *frisson* comes from the real or threatened gross invasion of the privacy of 'decent' people by violent men, an invasion in which rape as well as murder may be a real possibility. (On a larger scale, movies like Kazan's *The Wild Ones* and Kurosawa's *Seven Samurai* also belong there.) The situation is one that has always carried a sizeable emotional charge, but it was obviously felt with special intensity in the 1960s, as witness Pamela Hansford Johnson's particular indignation in *On Iniquity* about David Mercer's television play 'For Tea on Sunday', in which 'a young lout intrudes upon a perfectly harmless, if stuffy, middle-class group in their home, and proceeds to smash that home up with an axe. . . .'[3] And I think part of the intensity comes from the fact that the situation is especially likely to be charged with ambiguous feelings these days.

Rape itself, traditionally the perquisite of victorious invaders, is one of the most insidiously fascinating, if least discussed, of the more unpleasant human activities. Indeed, the fact that it *is* so little discussed is obviously an important reason for its fascination. In Hemingway's 'A Way You'll Never Be', the narrator mentions coming upon 'propaganda postcards showing a soldier . . . bending a woman backward over a bed; the figures were impressionistically drawn; very attractively depicted and had nothing in common with actual rape in which the woman's skirts are pulled over her head to smother her, one's comrade sometimes sitting on the head'. The physical realities of being violently raped are virtually never talked about publicly, least of all by the victims.[4]

17

The anonymous *A Woman of Berlin*, about the 1945 Russian occupation of that city,[5] must be unique both in the lucidity and dignity with which its author recognizes that submitting repeatedly to the conquerors was something that had to be endured without self-hatred as a natural feature of such an occupation, and in her acknowledgment that after a while the abrasion became physically very painful. More often than not, rape episodes arouse the discreditable suspicion that women end by getting pleasure from the experience.[6] This fantasy has revealed itself in a wide variety of works, such as best-sellers like E. M. Hull's *The Sheik*, and cartoons in men's magazines (e.g., the lady explorer carried off by the gorilla), and straight thrillers like *No Orchids for Miss Blandish*, and highbrow ones like Faulkner's *Sanctuary* and John Hawkes' *The Lime Twig*.[7] And it has received a good deal of intellectual corroboration in the last few years with the relaxation of censorship and the increasing availability of French erotica.

For various reasons, the most important of which is probably the influence and prestige of Sade, most of the classic erotic French novels appear to celebrate cruelty.[8] Despite talk about *le vice anglais*, and Swinburne's effusions, and the Soho kind of spanking-and-bondage books, the few substantial British erotic works of any distinction, such as John Cleland's *Memoirs of a Woman of Pleasure*, *Lady Chatterley's Lover*, and the pseudo-Byronic *Don Leon*, contain virtually no cruelty, while the 'prestige' American ones, like *Candy*, usually purport to be humorous.[9] But Sade's *Justine*, *Juliette*, *La philosophie dans le boudoir*, and *Les cent vingt jours de Sodome*, Musset's *Gamiani*, Apollinaire's *Les onze milles verges*, Octave Mirbeau's *Le jardin des supplices*, Georges Bataille's *Histoire d'un oeil*, and Réage's *Histoire d'O* all feature cruelty prominently, and so, to judge from Louis

18

Perceau's *Bibliographie du roman érotique au XIXe
siècle*,[10] do a good many other works. Novels like Andrea
de Nerciat's *Le diable au corps* and 'P.L.'s' *Trois filles de
leur mère* are noteworthy exceptions, but even in the
latter the overcoming of natural resistances and revul-
sions is prominent. Moreover, a curious kind of moralistic
note sometimes enters into the treatment of violation in
French works. As Maurice Blanchot points out, 'For Sade,
sovereign man is impervious to evil because no one can do
him any harm. He is a man possessed of every passion,
and his passions are slaked by any and everything. . . .
The absolute egoist is he who is able to transform everything disagreeable into something likable, everything
repugnant into something attractive. . . . If he injures
others, the result is voluptuous; injury endured at their
hands is sheer delight. . . . If he lives, there is no circum-
stance, no event that he cannot turn into happiness.'[11]
And the almost religious benefits of being violated were
celebrated in apotheosis in the mid-1950s in *Histoire d'O*,
the moral authority of which was enhanced not only by
Jean Paulhan's afterword but by the near-certainty that
the author was a woman.[12]

In other words, the dice have been loaded where rape
is concerned. Graphics like Goya's *Los Desastros de la
Guerra* and Käthe Kollwitz's 'Raped and Abandoned' are
very rare; and even the sickening multiple-rape episode
in Selby's *The Room*, unparalleled as it is in its fulness
and physicality, has an equivocal misogynous tinge.

Where attitudes towards the victims of violation of one
kind or another are concerned, this pattern obviously
deserves to be viewed with suspicion. It is true that for
the most part the French intellectuals who have been
most enthusiastic about Sade appear to have been
honourably and unequivocally opposed to anything
resembling Fascism and to the sickening torture that went

on in French Algeria. But there are still dangers lurking in things like Paulhan's afterword to *Histoire d'O*, with its celebration of those happier times when criminals were 'boldly' executed in public and husbands had the right to beat their wives. Just as gangster movies can subtly influence one's reaction to non-fictional presentations of gangsters, so it seems to me that if one comes to accounts of the Algerian tortures, such as those in Henri Alleg's *La question*, or the anonymously compiled *La gangrène*, or Simone de Beauvoir and Gisele Halimi's *Djamila Boupacha*,[13] after reading the works that I have talked about, one's responses may not be quite as resolute and unequivocal as they might be. It is always possible to misuse true accounts of atrocities, after all. D. H. Lawrence, for example, discussing the flogging episode in Henry Dana's *Two Years before the Mast*, could exclaim fatuously, 'Why shall man not be whipped? As long as man has a bottom, he must surely be whipped. It is as if the Lord intended it so. . . . I would rather be flogged than have most people "like" me.'[14] However, what interests me more at this point are certain instabilities in our attitudes towards the figure of the violator, especially the violator-as-outsider.

The gangster, as he figures in the gangster movie, may be outside legitimate society, but he is still almost invariably someone inextricably involved *with* society. He is trying to make his way to power and prestige inside the Mob, or Organization, or Syndicate, if he doesn't already have it at the outset of the movie; and even if, as in a movie like Boorman's *Point Blank*, he is a maverick, the Organization still has pride of place in his aspirations and fears. In the violation movie, on the other hand, the potential or actual violator is defined for us very largely in terms of his relationship to his victims. I mean that that relationship gives him for us most of his moral or intellectual significance. In that relationship, further-more, he is frequently a man in the grip of an obsession or craving, a man who is either consciously bent on the violation or destruction of innocents or who is so estranged by generalized resentments that dealing with him is like trying to deal with a time-bomb. And an almost numinous aura has frequently surrounded the figure of the *enragé*, whether the berserker in battle, or the demonic bar-room brawler, or the ghetto rioter in a state of incandescent fury, or any of a number of fictional figures at certain moments – Heathcliff in *Wuthering Heights*, for example, or Goulay in George Douglas's *The House with the Green Shutters*, or Macbeth at the end of the play, or Dmitri Karamazov. I do not mean that the figures in the kind of violation movie that I am talking about possess that kind of dignity. But the aura surround-ing the literally enraged man, or the kind of man liable to fearful rages, comes not only from fear or from the fact that the great majority of people are incapable of losing their self-consciousness in an intensity of passion, but also from the ancient association of 'possession' and 'vision'. And the uncertainty as to whether there may not be something to be said even for states of 'clinical' mad-ness has received a good deal of reinforcement in this century, whether in the Surrealists' celebration of that 'dérèglement systématique de tous les sens' ('systematic derangement of all the senses') that Rimbaud spoke of, or in more or less Dionysiac readings of novelists like Dostoevsky and Faulkner, or in the writings of R. D. Laing.

Moreover, for a considerable time now, there has also been the notion of the criminal as saint, or seer, or artist to contend with. Partly this arises from the phenomenon of criminals who themselves display remarkable extremes of violent criminality and genuine devoutness, Gilles de

Rais being the paradigmatic example. Partly it comes from other situations in which the complex intensities and anguishes of the perpetrator of a crime (Othello, for example, or a good many actual perpetrators of *crimes passionels*), or the complexities of the situation in which the crime occurs (e.g., Hamlet's killing of Polonius), are such that it becomes difficult to see the figure as a criminal at all. Partly too it comes from philosophical or quasi-philosophical endeavours, whether by Nietzsche, or Sade, or Genet, to demonstrate the awfulness of 'normal' social behaviour in such a way that the much more limited destructiveness of the genuinely risk-taking outlaw looks good in comparison. Whatever the validity of the reasons, the psychological fact is that these days – as the cult-esteem that has been accorded figures like Charles Manson and Hell's Angels shows – the criminal, particularly the invading or violating criminal, is likely to be viewed as ambivalently as certain kinds of victims are, at least when one appears in no danger of becoming a victim oneself. In some ways this kind of tolerance towards criminals may be thought to be merely a continuation of the tradition that the *Time* reviewer referred to when he spoke of Americans' tendency to see gangsters as 'individualistic resistance fighters against society' – the Robin Hood tradition, the Jesse James tradition, the Ned Kelly tradition. But what is new is a much greater self-projection than before into the figure of the psychopath or at least a certain kind of psychopath.

Confronted with figures like Charles Starkweather and his girl friend, who casually did to death ten strangers in the course of an interstate car-trip, or Smith and Hickock of *In Cold Blood* fame, or the Manson 'family', it is natural enough to feel, in one's horror, that these are quintessentially modern examples of anomie and alienation. But the homicidal career of the fearsome Harpe brothers in Tennessee around the end of the eighteenth century appears to have been just as pathological and gratuitous, as well as far more destructive;[15] and no doubt there have been a good many other figures that could be adduced from among the badmen of the American West and other violent groups. Nevertheless, it is understandable that such figures should inspire the peculiar dread that they do nowadays. It is not merely the sense of the utter unreachableness of the criminal at the moment of the crime (unreachableness by any appeal that the victims could have made, or that we ourselves could have made had we been in their positions) that makes so dreadful the thought of Smith and Hickock in the Clutters' house, or of the wholesome-looking young women of the Manson family chattering and laughing during their trial. Behind such instances lies the supreme instance of large-scale schizophrenic unreachableness in recorded history, namely the activities of the S.S. men and other functionaries engaged in the business of extermination in German-occupied Europe. And behind that in turn lies the philosophical and moral alienation and anomie explored by such very different writers as Conrad, Dostoevsky, Hemingway, Kafka, and Camus – a philosophical nihilism which it is peculiarly tempting for a good many people to see not simply as one philosophical position among a number of others, but as a revelation to us of *the* truth about the human condition.

Hence the peculiar kind of discomfort that it was possible to feel during the enthusiastic reception of Truman Capote's *In Cold Blood*. When one read the reviews and looked at the photographs accompanying some of them, it was the murdered family that seemed remote and slightly unreal; the two killers, in contrast, emerged from the pages as interestingly disturbed nihilistic beings of a kind closer to intellectuals and more intellectually acceptable than the sort of Kansas farmer who goes willingly to church socials. Ambivalence of this sort suggests that one might, if faced with a comparable menace, act with a good deal less than the decisiveness necessary for one's own preservation and the preservation of others – i.e., that one might be already too close for comfort to the position of Axel Heyst in Conrad's *Victory* after the landing of the murderous trio on his island refuge. It is all too possible even for non-intellectuals to suffer from a similar debility, as Diana Trilling reminded us in her discussion of Capote's book.[16] After all, part of the disquieting aspect of the *In Cold Blood* murders, and even more of the butchering of the eight young nurses in their own Chicago apartment by Richard Speck, was the signal failure of the victims to do anything effective in their own defence. And latent in such a failure lurks, I think, the insidious question whether some larger failure of will and imagination may not have been going on, a loss of the kinds of images of existence that can energize one to the highest degree of self-preservative action.

However, it is intellectuals that principally concern me here; and one of the most significant developments in the past two or three decades (in fiction it goes back to Camus' *L'Étranger*, I suppose) is the way in which certain presentations in art reinforce and in a sense confirm the psychopathological vision of the violators, especially in movies. And it was because of this, I think, that the coldly clever rape scene in *A Clockwork Orange* was felt to be so much more disturbing even than the one in *Straw Dogs*, which was chiefly an illustration of the conventional male myth about the raped female (she asked for it). The interior of the secluded house in *A Clockwork Orange* hinted at a somewhat artificial evasion of unpleasant social realities by the married

24

couple, so that with the invasion by the three figures in masquerade costumes there was a feeling of appropriateness both in the ironic confrontation of quasi-doubles and in the implacable entry of those realities. The use of a hand-held camera stylistically supported the aggressiveness of the invaders. The burlesque-elegant snipping away of the wife's jumpsuit began by making it seem as if she too were in fancy-dress, a partner in a curious ritual, and ended by leaving her looking like a large denuded doll. And the soft-shoe dancing and much-commented-on singing of 'Singin' in the Rain' was not only a further instance of the conversion of life into artifice by the hero but, with its distancing allusion to the Donen–Kelly classic of that title, helped to turn the whole episode into 'cinema'. By the end of the sequence the wife and husband had virtually disappeared as suffering consciousness. It was hard to believe later on that the kicking of the husband had been brutal enough to cripple him and even harder to believe that the wife died because of what had been done to her, the rape itself having shrewdly not been shown at all. And the subsequent murder of the cat-loving sculptress, with its literally phallic murder weapon and its even more withdrawn and self-regarding victim, was simply more of the same, a rape-substitute in the same alienated and alienating style, so that the whole first part of the movie became emotionally ambiguous. As I said, one can see why the movie should have been found disquieting.

However, where our uneasiness about the psychopathic is concerned, there seem to me to have been some further factors at work. The American source for the kind of aestheticizing and distancing of violence in *A Clockwork Orange* is plain enough: it is *Bonnie and Clyde*. And the European source is no less clear: it is the earlier movies of Jean-Luc Godard. The implications lead one deeper into what may be called the collective intellectual psyche of our time.

It was piquant that in an interview Godard should have declared that he found *Bonnie and Clyde* detestable. His dislike of it was understandable, of course. For all its air of protest, particularly in its handling of the implacable and unpleasant peace-officer who hounded the couple, and the overkill gunning-down of them at the end, the movie was as little a genuine work of protest as the kind of full-page colour ad in which a moneyed young couple are Getting Away From It All on a tropical beach somewhere or other. What Penn was really doing in his treatment of the American 1930s, with his knowing references to the images of impoverished rural decency in works like Lange's and Evans' photographs and Ford's *The Grapes of Wrath*, his contrasting allusions to silent movie comedy, and his patronizing or derisive attitude to the 'square' figures in the non-documentary parts, was declaring independence from all the earnest, socially conscious demands that still lingered on from that period. He did so, however, so far as could be discerned, in the name of nothing more than the cult of the Beautiful (Rich) Young People. Technically the Bonnie and Clyde of the movie may not have been rich. But as the fashion-designers recognized almost immediately, they were Gatsby and Daisy, and Scott and Zelda, and all the other charmers who had looks and style, and rode around with casual recklessness in open cars, and insouciantly disregarded 'ordinary' people, and didn't *worry* about things, and had sunny weather all the way. And since their victims were a set of walking clichés whose deaths could disturb no one, even their violences were fun. It is not surprising that the movie should have been extremely popular, and since its influence obviously made possible such other period reconstructions as Smith's lovingly crafted and poetic *The Travelling Executioner*, and Scorsese's genuinely radical *Boxcar Bertha*, as well as bringing a new kind of *plein-air* charm into a good many other movies, one can be grateful for it. But it was a duplicitous piece of work nonetheless, and its makers were obviously running far fewer risks than Godard himself had done, especially in *À bout de souffle*, in which, far from reducing all the square settings to cliché and 'cinema', he juxtaposed his own outlaws with a remarkably real and unstereotyped Paris.

The irony, however, is that it was nevertheless from *À bout de souffle* that Penn had derived most of his basic attitudes and strategies. And what especially characterized that remarkable work was the coincidence between the killer's moral indifference and the vision of the movie as a whole that I have been talking about. The murder itself was brilliantly converted into 'fiction' by being presented in exactly the kind of B-movie preview technique that the hero must have seen a great many specimens of in the course of his movie-going career. The murdered man was dehumanized still further by the subsequent witty disruption of stereotypes in the presentation of the other policemen. And the result was that for almost the whole movie one could give oneself up, if one wished, to sharing Godard's uncritical enjoyment of the pretty-boy killer's everyday activities. For the hero, in effect, the murder virtually didn't exist, hadn't happened, didn't *matter* in the least; he was simply a normal young man with much more serious problems to think about, such as money and Jean Seberg. And to be drawn sympathetically into this kind of vision and this kind of 'banality of evil' (to use Hannah Arendt's phrase) is a serious matter. Such a benumbing of the moral faculties, moreover, is central to Godard's work and influence, and has clear historical roots. What is involved is an instability of attitude that goes back to the Second World War, and I suspect that many of us are still suffering from it.

In *Lions and Shadows*, Christopher Isherwood speaks of the consequences of having been an adolescent during the 1914–18 war:

> Like most of my generation, I was obsessed [in the 1920s] by a complex of terrors and longings connected with the idea 'War'. 'War', in this purely neurotic sense, meant The Test. The test of your courage, of your maturity, of your sexual prowess: 'Are you really a Man?' Subconsciously, I believe, I longed to be subjected to this test; but I also dreaded failure. I dreaded failure so much – indeed, I was so certain that I *should* fail – that, consciously, I denied my longing to be tested altogether. I denied my all-consuming morbid interest in the idea of 'war'. I pretended indifference. The War, I said, was obscene, not even thrilling, a nuisance, a bore. (ch. 2.)

A good deal of Godard's own odd empty energy comes, it seems to me, from his belonging to a generation old enough during the Second World War to be required to *feel* intensely, but not old enough to be required to act, and for whom the horrors existed almost entirely at second-hand. In two of his best novels, *Date with Darkness* and *The Steel Mirror*, Donald Hamilton explores the consciousness of the kind of intelligent American, never himself on active service, for whom, as for many of us, the quintessential moral image in that war was France under the Gestapo – a situation in which some of the most appalling atrocities took place in the most civilized of countries, and in which intelligent and sensitive people were confronted daily, from 1942 or so onwards, with the moral obligation to resist the occupiers and with the terrible question of how they would be likely to behave if caught.[17] And I suspect that it is in some such terms that one can account for the curiously uneasy relationship to 'official' culture, and the concern in one way or another with extreme situations and physical or moral violences, that one sees in a number of Anglo-American intellectuals of Godard's generation, such figures as George Steiner, A. Alvarez, and Thom Gunn. While they were growing up, traditional culture was one of the things that energized the struggle against barbarism, and as the war began to go in favour of the Allies it became possible to concentrate on the examination-passing business of trying to enter the world of that culture oneself, since the odds were that one would still be alive when the war ended. But the alternative vision still remained of a world in which all the books and galleries and concert-halls, all the genteel rituals of art and the academic life, were irrelevant in comparison with the question of how one would comport oneself in the torture chambers of the Gestapo, or behind the barbed wire of Dachau or Auschwitz.

At the same time, this was a highly artificial position to be in. Part of the distinction and interest of the two novels by Hamilton is his facing, in the immediate post-war world, the fact that one *didn't* know what the actuality had been like, and that almost inescapably 'it always turned out Hollywood when you tried to imagine it. You knew it had not been like that, but you had no idea of how it really had been. When they said "underground" and "Gestapo" it came out Warner Brothers, passed by the state board of censors.'[18] And I think that, paradoxically, things were made harder, and the claims on one's feelings more oppressive, as media-records of the Nazi atrocities became increasingly available, especially if one was still adolescent. What was required of one was a hyper-intensity of response to situations that were beyond one's grasp except in the grossest terms of Monsters versus Heroic Innocents. And as one matured beyond the point where the simple stereotypes could satisfy, one was left with a growing blankness when faced with the media-records. It was virtually impossible to transpose those skeletal, insect-like, grey creatures of the concentration-camp photographs back into former office-managers taking the train to work, guests at wedding parties, holiday-makers sunbathing, mothers setting their daughters' hair, and so on – back, in other words, into the everyday normalities of their former existence. And where some of their tormentors are concerned, it has been difficult more recently to transpose the exposed and arrested brewery managers or general practitioners or public-relations men back into either the monsters of wartime propaganda or the more alarming kind of monsters of actuality, they being now so incapable, apparently, of conceiving of themselves in either role; conceiving of themselves, I mean, as having behaved monstrously or abnormally in any way at all.

Hence, I think, the peculiar significance of Godard's work. During the 1950s one became increasingly conscious both that what was displayed in atrocity photographs and newsreels was the most dreadful affront to civilized values imaginable, and that nevertheless one's reactions were becoming dulled. Resnais tackled the phenomenon head on in *Nuit et brouillard* and, where other atrocities were concerned, in *Hiroshima mon amour*; and the first of these two movies, at least, is among the masterpieces of cinema. Almost as revealing in some ways, however, was the little episode in Godard's *Une femme mariée* in which a friend just back from a trip East tells the empty-headed adultering heroine that he visited a trial going on at Auschwitz (I quote from memory) and she, vaguely inferring from his tone that some significance is intended, ventures indifferently, 'Oh – Thalidomide?' 'No, the concentration camps.' 'Oh' (indifferently and incuriously), and the subject is dropped. What Godard himself has done, it seems to me, has been defiantly to refuse to feel guilty about the failures of imagination and sympathy that I have been talking about, and to make a film career during most of the 1960s out of conceiving of violent situations in which intense feelings are normally involved and demanded – a cop-killer on the run, a nice girl becoming a prostitute and getting killed by hoodlums, wartime atrocities, political assassinations, tortures, and so on – and then refusing to feel strongly about them himself or to create characters who do so. It is probably for this reason that his films have been so popular in England; the strains and bafflements that I have been speaking of were especially strong there. The fact that in the States the movies of Antonioni were more popular than Godard's at first, particularly with academics, suggests that what was felt more acutely as oppressive there for a while as salaries rose were the 1930s radical tradition of an austere disdain for success in the bourgeois world, and the related tradition of a we-two-against-the-world's-corruptions kind of love.[19]

Moreover, this pattern of initial overstrain and subsequent collapse and renunciation has been observable in one or two other areas too, and they bear on the kind of shift in the early 1960s that I have talked about. The crucial emergence of Pop, for example, clearly resulted from the felt tyranny of the Abstract Expressionist demand for an intensity of feeling and a purity of self-abandonment that were hard enough to attain to anyway even for someone like Willem de Kooning, and that were becoming increasingly difficult for younger artists to strive for when they contemplated the actual thinness and deadness of the work of some of the people to whom these qualities had been attributed and who were being rewarded accordingly. But it was also a reaction to the general intensities called for in what Susan Sontag in *Against Interpretation* called 'the culturally over-saturated medium in which contemporary sensibility is schooled' (p. 288). The peculiar fascination of Roy Lichtenstein's earlier paintings, for example, was not only that they drew attention to the surface antithesis and deeper resemblances between the Blam Splat Pow violences of the action comics and the *True Romances* kind of vapidity. The dehumanizations of the comic books were themselves presented in his work in an emotionally empty and dehumanized way, so that the deeper appeal was to people who were worried not so much by the violence and vapidity themselves as by their own inability to be worried by them enough. They were paintings for people for whom the illustrations in *Seduction of the Innocent* (itself, as Warshow shrewdly noted, 'a kind of crime comic book for parents') had become a drag, just as Warhol's graphics were graphics for people for whom all the indignation about commercialism had become a drag.

And the appeal of McLuhan's *Understanding Media* was obviously of much the same kind. On the one hand it was a relief to be informed that the supposed arch-enemy of culture, commercial television, had in reality been making for sweetness and light all along, and that virtually all the cultural commentators in this century had been in error in calling for a vigilantly critical attitude towards commercialism. And on the other hand, there was the reassuring aplomb with which a genuine authenticated university professor had abandoned such things as sustained and rational argument, a conscientious interrogation of sources, an endeavour to discriminate as precisely as possible between different manifestations of the 'same' thing (e.g., television talk-shows), an alertness to exceptions that might call for a recasting of one's formulations, a readiness to attend carefully to the arguments of opponents and argue carefully with them, an implicit acknowledgment that there might be limits somewhere to one's own knowledge, insight, and understanding, and a style capable of registering such emotions as anger, affection, esteem, puzzlement, sympathy, disgust, outrage – in sum, the abandonment of most of the features thought of as desirable if one were trying to live intensely the life of the mind. It was all very reassuring, especially if one aspired to intellectuality of a sort oneself and had been made to feel inferior and unworthy by the Columbia College kind of high culture – *Das Kapital* and *The City of God* for duty, *The Golden Bowl* for pleasure, and the review pages of the *Partisan Review* for delight, to adapt a naughty Arab saying.

The developments that I have been speaking of bring to mind Huizinga's comment in *The Waning of the Middle Ages* that 'This spiritual wakefulness . . . results in a dangerous state of tension, for the presupposed transcendental feelings are sometimes dormant, and whenever this is the case, all that is meant to stimulate spiritual consciousness is reduced to appalling commonplace profanity, to a startling worldliness in other-worldly guise.'[20] They are understandable; in retrospect they may have been inescapable; and in some ways they have probably even been desirable, in the sense that some of the strains that people were trying to cope with earlier were excessive and in some measure artificial. If the 1960s was a decade of relaxations of various kinds, however, and of a new omnivorousness, it was also one that demonstrated the essential truth of Remy de Gourmont's caution at the start of the century:

If a civilized country should arrive one day at that state of mind in which every novelty is immediately welcomed and enthroned in the place of traditional ideas and mechanisms – if the past were to yield constantly to the future – then, after a period of frenzied curiosity, we would see men falling into the apathy of the tourist who never looks twice at the same thing. In order to regain possession of themselves, they would have to seek refuge in a purely animal existence, and civilization would perish.[21]

And from this point of view it is significant that the strategy of defiantly refusing to feel anything sharp and clear while playing in a game where feeling is conventionally demanded has become a standard feature of a sizeable part of the art scene. Indeed, the whole progression from Pop, through Op, through minimal art, to the various forms of non-art and anti-art, seems to have consisted substantially of devising situations in which such a refusal continues to be possible and can, it is hoped, still induce at least a *frisson* of initial indignation in the more historical-minded viewer, *avant-garde* art having become almost by definition something that such a viewer is annoyed by. One has the impression that for McLuhan, similarly, the chief problem since *Understanding Media* has been to find new ways to be annoying to the people annoyed by *Understanding Media*, which, since he was principally annoying in the first place by virtue of the intellectual and rhetorical decencies that he didn't observe and the humane emotions that he couldn't or wouldn't feel, has resulted in a progressive coarsening and thinning of utterance. And the same pattern, for that matter, seems observable in the more recent works of Godard, such as *Pravda*.

Understandable as it may be, however, emotional emptiness is still emotional emptiness, even when it is the result of intellectual combat-fatigue; and this emptiness and the entailed indifferences and dehumanizations seem to me to have been the prime enemy in the 1960s and still a very real danger. Indeed, the very intensity of the dramatic events during the later 1960s seems likely, if anything, to have increased the probability of it, because of the new kinds of psychic overloading that were going on. The War, the Ghettoes, the Moonshots, Biafra, McLuhanism, Woman's Lib, the Drug Scene, Czechoslovakia, the War, the Steps of the Pentagon, the People's Park, the Kent State killings, Woodstock, the War, the Panthers, Free Schools, Be-Ins, Abortion, Bangladesh, Full Frontal Nudity, Gay Lib, Bussing, Pornography, Ecology, the War, the War, the War, the War (puffs, powders, patches, Bibles, billet-doux) – the very fact that such a list, with behind it so much misery and so many crimes, should appear already faded and dated suggests the difficulty of coping emotionally with such a plethora of information and argument. Even at the best of times, one is always in danger of lapsing into indifference towards subjects that one cannot afford to be indifferent to; it can be a welcome relief to escape from the pain of consciousness. But if the medieval Church indeed considered accidie one of the gravest of sins, it was surely right.

Moreover, the other side of the coin that I have been talking about, particularly in America, may be the wrong kind of liking for violence of one kind or another on the part of people still going through the liberal motions but fundamentally bored or constricted by them and craving variety and release. Hannah Arendt has spoken in *The*

Origins of Totalitarianism of the growing fascination with 'underworlds' of a fin-de-siècle Paris high society 'constantly on the lookout for the strange, the exotic, the dangerous'.[22] It is obvious enough that part of the fascination of the Black Panthers in liberal New York for a while had less to do with the real history of American Blacks, as set out, for example, in Gunnar Myrdal's *An American Dilemma*, or with the arguments of books like Stokely Carmichael and Charles V. Hamilton's *Black Power*, Eldridge Cleaver's *Soul on Ice*, and Frantz Fanon's *The Wretched of the Earth*, than it did with the fact that, as presented by the Press, the Panthers were big bad black men who wore leather and carried guns. That is, they were degraded to being a few rungs up the ladder from figures like Hell's Angels (the sentimentalizing of whom led to the murderous fiasco of the Altamont rock festival) or the kind of leather-jacketed, heavy-booted 'rough trade' that attracts a certain kind of homosexual. So too, at a much higher level, with the *volte-face* of a lot of American peaceniks during the 1967 Israeli-Arab war, napalm and all. It was not simply the fact of Israel's fighting for its survival that made that episode so emotion-charged; it was also the fact that the brilliant Israeli general staff were so obviously *winners*, in the peculiarly resonant American sense of that term.[23] There had obviously for a number of years previously been an excessive tension in a good many liberal minds, especially Jewish minds, between the kind of official niceness that I spoke of earlier and the kind of yearning that got into print in the late 1930s in Irwin Shaw's short story 'Sailor Off the Bremen', as in a passage like the following apropos of the beating up by Leftists of a Nazi ashore in New York who had blinded one of their comrades in one eye:

Charley [the brother of the injured man] worked very

methodically, getting his two hundred pounds behind
short, accurate, smashing blows. . . . When he got
through with the nose, Charley went after the mouth,
hooking along the side of the jaw with both hands,
until teeth fell out and the jaw hung open, smashed,
loose with the queer looseness of flesh that is no longer
moored to solid bone. . . .

When he started on Lueger's eye, Charley talked.
'You bastard. Oh, you lousy goddamn bastard', came
out with the sobs and the tears as he hit at the eye
with his right hand, cutting it, smashing it, tearing it
again and again, his hand coming away splattered
with blood each time. . . . And he kept hitting with
fury and deliberation at the shattered eye.

It wasn't altogether surprising that Nathan Glazer
should have felt able to observe in *Commentary* in 1969
that 'I do not want to deprive blacks of all the credit for
the mood of violence that hangs over the country and
frightens almost everyone, but we must acknowledge
that white intellectuals, and that . . . means in large
measure Jewish intellectuals, have taught violence, justi-
fied violence, rationalized violence.'[24] Nor, for that
matter, is it surprising that there should have been so
much ambivalence and uncertainty in the attitudes of
academics towards campus disturbances – ambivalance
and uncertainty, that is, in excess of the obvious complexity of the whole problem. Most people enjoy watching
conflagrations, as E. M. Forster noted of the Nazi book-
burnings,[25] and even academics, with part of their mind,
are capable of relishing the thought of a squad of militants sending the whole monstrous card catalogue of the
Widener Library at Harvard up in flames. One of the
sadder, because symptomatic, touches during the strike
at San Francisco State College was a youngish professor

of English ('I was a good boy in the academy, a graduate of Harvard, I even wrote three books, always a good academic boy') explaining how, during his alliance with the students, he had felt *alive*.[26]

It should be borne in mind, furthermore, that if the favourite British double-life story is that epitomized in the Scarlet Pimpernel books (the fop who is secretly a hero), the favourite American one is Superman. And there is nothing heroic about Superman at all; his whole appeal is that he doesn't even have to *try* to be heroic; he is simply invulnerable from the start, and, being infallibly on the side of right, can use whatever violences he wishes. On a small scale, the dark side of the liberal ability to veer from a priggish pacificism and exaggerated 'tolerance' to an excessive use of force once the morality light has gone on[27] is explored in *Straw Dogs* – a movie that makes sense only if one recognizes that Peckinpah should really have set his milquetoast academic down in the American South and given him his chance to prove his manhood gorily against the feared and hated rednecks of that region. On a much larger scale, I fear, a substantial part of the appeal of John Kennedy was precisely that beneath the good looks and the Harvard veneer he was as calculating and ruthless an operator as the youngest brother Michael in *The Godfather*, who, like him, had the advantage of belonging to a closely-knit family headed by a very wealthy and ruthless patriarch. It should also be kept in mind that while the great majority of the domestic violences in American history are clearly not defensible by liberal standards, the supreme domestic violence, namely the Civil War, was one in which, in the name of peace and freedom, force was used by the liberal North on a scale and with a thoroughness hitherto unprecedented. What Kennedy appears to have done was provide his palace liberals with an opportunity to engage in the *Realpolitik* of the Cold War with similarly clear consciences.[28] The emotional appeal of politic-military 'realism' should never be underestimated, either, as Orwell knew. And if the social injustices inside America and the disparities between America and the Third World countries became increasingly blatant and incongruous, it will no doubt grow stronger, at least for those whom the disparities favour and who grow increasingly reluctant to feel guilty about them.[29]

But if the reverse side of accidie is violence, this is partly because violence is felt to promise not merely a titillating but a radical relief from accidie. In the next chapter I shall glance at certain aspects of this belief where art is concerned.

REVOLT

If the increasing politicization of violence was one of the most exhausting aspects of the 1960s, it was also one that did most to increase sophistication in discussions of it. Faced in the States during the 1950s with the seemingly gratuitous violences of well-to-do young vandals, for example, it was difficult to do more than fall back on the notion of boredom or accidie as a cause, as Arthur Miller, for example, did when pondering the matter in 1962.[1] By the mid-1960s, when Norman Mailer was discussing violence in terms of an existential defence of the self, a demonstration that 'there is something in the center of nature itself which resists any social directive that life be not complex, not contradictory, not explosive, not full of ambush and reward',[2] the nature of the social structures working against those things where the young were concerned was becoming clearer in works like Paul Goodman's *Growing Up Absurd* and Edgar Z. Friedenberg's *Coming of Age in America*.[3] And by the end of the decade, Hannah Arendt, in her magnificent *On Violence*, was able to pass beyond the obvious political formulae and point to factors liable to obtain under any system, whatever its ostensible political colouring.

The following passage from that work seems to me of central importance where artistic as well as political violences are concerned:

If we inquire historically into the causes likely to

transform *engagés* into *enragés*, it is not injustice that
ranks first, but hypocrisy. . . . Not many authors of rank
glorified violence for violence's sake; but these few –
Sorel, Pareto, Fanon – were motivated by a much
deeper hatred of bourgeois society and were led to a
much more radical break with its moral standards than
the conventional Left, which was chiefly inspired by
compassion and a burning desire for justice. To tear
the mask of hypocrisy from the face of the enemy, to
unmask him and the devious machinations and
manipulations that permit him to rule without using
violent means, that is, to provoke action even at the
risk of annihilation so that the truth may come out –
these are still among the strongest motives in today's
violence on the campuses and in the streets. And this
violence . . . is not irrational. Since men live in a world
of appearances and, in their dealings with it, depend
on manifestation, hypocrisy's conceits – as distinguished
from expedient ruses, followed by disclosure in due
time – cannot be met by so-called reasonable
behavior. Words can be relied on only if one is sure
that their function is to reveal and not to conceal. It
is the semblance of rationality, much more than the
interests behind it, that provokes rage. To use
reason when reason is used as a trap is not 'rational';
just as to use a gun in self-defense is not
'irrational'.[4]

Years ago, Lawrence saw 'niceness' and pseudo-reason-
ableness as game-rules that permit would-be dominators
to put the burden of guilt on those who are being
dominated. It should not be forgotten that most of the
students involved in the various 'confrontations' in the
States were born in the late 1940s and early 1950s, and
that during the years in which they were growing to

consciousness the adult cult of a homogenized niceness was more powerful than ever before.

And it is obvious in retrospect how the same nexus of things in the first half of the 1960s that invited political violences also invited aesthetic ones. The increasingly obvious bureaucratization of society, the evasion of personal responsibility by many of those in positions of authority (especially in institutions of learning), the use of 'reasonableness' as a means of dominance and manipulation, the attempted promotion of an unnatural and stultifying urbanity of behaviour and feeling, the increasingly chi-chi formalism alike of gallery art, fashion, and advertising, the cult of the Beautiful (Rich) People, the speed with which developments in the arts were appropriated for purely commercial ends, the unparalleled reduction of art to objects to be 'consumed' by the well-to-do (a Henry Moore statuette, an Art Nouveau ash-tray, a Campbell's Soup can all equally art 'objects'), the increasing pseudo-tolerance and unshockableness that derived from the unspoken conviction that nothing could any longer seriously disrupt the pattern of business growth, technological imperialism, and the professionalization of the intelligent young – contemplating these and allied phenomena, the legitimacy in principle of the various efforts to break the pattern during that decade seems hardly open to question. It is easy enough, therefore, to see why violence should have come to be seen in terms of an escape, a release, an intense self-affirmation, whether by individuals or groups; or, relatedly, as a way of forcing people to truth. And one can see too why, during the 1960s, the older artists who seemed in some ways to answer the most fully to human needs, revolutionary human needs, were what might be called explosive ones – Céline, Genet, Strindberg, Bacon, Artaud, Goya, Sade, Buñuel, and so on – and why the violences in more popular works should start to acquire a revolutionary nimbus. At the same time, there were obvious opportunities for confusion here.

In this connection, Steve Carpenter's 'Who's Who in the New Cult of Violence' in the June 1969 issue of *Rogue* magazine made particularly interesting reading. Not only figures like Ché Guevara, Danny the Red and Bobby Seale, it appeared, were cult or culture heroes. So too were ones like Hell's Angels, Jim Morrison (of The Doors), the ultra-violent comic-book character The Hulk, and even the colourless young mass-murderer Charles Starkweather. And it was obvious that more was involved than a naive enthusiasm for violent or aggressive people of one kind or another. The figures also fitted into a certain conception of art, with Acid-Rock, Happenings, the later movies of Godard, and the rest of the art-activities that involve sensory overloading or deprivation. I am referring to the view of art in which there is a simple dichotomy between oppressive 'order' and liberating 'revolt', and in which the latter term is applied honorifically to art-activities that do violence to the sensibilities of people thought to be on the side of order, frequently by means of the violation of taboos.[5]

It seems to me, however, that to conceive of revolutionary art in such terms is as simplistic as it is to conceive of 'traditional' art in terms of the observance of rules. And this is particularly obvious where violence in the theatre is concerned. I am thinking of the kind of approach, involving a gross misreading of Artaud, that sees the essential nature of the theatrical enterprise as having been defined in the relationship between performer and audience that obtained in the Nouveau Théâtre on 10 December 1896, when Firmin Gémier pronounced the opening word of Jarry's *Ubu Roi*: 'Merdre!' But if theatrical violences, even when they escalated, were losing their power to shock during the later 1960s, this was not only because of social changes outside the theatre. It was also because theatre audiences, like the young watching television violences, were reading more accurately the conventions and game-rules involved. Not only is the theatrical language for representing gougings, whippings, maimings, and so on relatively thin and stereotyped if the director and actors are of only middling talent. Much more to the point is that the 'cruelty' play easily becomes established as a genre, either because the author has conceived the work in that way, or because several directors have been emphasizing cruelties in their productions.[6] Hence the author or director may begin by postulating a deservedly shockable bourgeois audience, but ends up with an audience that is begging for shocks to be given it, either because it identifies with the artist against 'society' or because it is slumming. And even if escalation is attempted, the new language is rapidly learned, the limits of the expectable expand, the hitherto taboo is commended by society itself in the name of art,[7] and it all becomes once more the same old art game as, say, the Grand Guignol Theatre used to be, with the added titillation for the audience of thinking that occasionally, as with strip-teasers in the days when they still raided burlesque houses, the performers may *really* expose themselves to prosecution. The only thing left that would be likely to elicit reprisals, both critical and legal, would be the actual mistreatment of the innocent and helpless; and the reprisals would be merited, even in *avant-garde* terms, because of the complicity involved. Some things do defile; the episode in Fellini's *Satyricon* in which, in the course of a theatrical 'performance' in Imperial Rome, an imbecile's hand is deliberately lopped off is a study in defilement.[8]

44

At the same time it is obvious that violences can indeed help at times to make the theatre, in Artaud's words in *The Theatre and Its Double*, 'a believable reality which gives the heart and the senses that kind of concrete bite which all true sensation requires' (p. 85).[9] And it is therefore important to distinguish between two ways in which the ostensibly outrageous can be disturbing. It would indeed be disturbing to watch someone killing an animal on stage. It is disturbing, even if not very arousing, to observe someone engaging in fellatio on stage without giving any sign of being bothered by being watched. It is disturbing to be part of a Happening organized and directed by someone who combines desolating banality of vision and poverty of invention with inordinate self-conceit. But the common denominator of these experiences is that one is involved temporarily with modes of consciousness in which certain kinds of collapse have occurred or in which certain kinds of psychic impoverishment are all too visible, and which are largely sealed off from normal social ones. And to be a spectator at such events is to be drawn temporarily away from larger structures of thought and values, and shut up inside the walls of the theatre, or wherever it is, with a confusion and thinning-out of one's own normal consciousness.

The exact opposite happens with a genuinely revolutionary work like the Living Theatre's production of Kenneth H. Brown's *The Brig*, one of the most distinguished and, in Artaud's sense, 'cruellest' theatrical events that has occurred in America. One was intensely conscious of being present in a particular place for a particular length of time: part of the cruelty lay precisely in one's being unable to escape for a moment from the real time occupied by these actors stamping their feet, yelling at the top of their voices their request to cross the white line – SIR! – frantically dressing and undressing on command, scrubbing the floor, moving constantly at the double, and so on. But these actors, by performing these actions so rigorously, were also in part *becoming* prisoners in a U.S. Marine Corps detention area, and so were pointing one outside towards the consciousness of actual prisoners in such places. The actors playing the NCOs, too, pointed one out towards the consciousness of men who would willingly serve in such a capacity. And beyond that were the Marine Corps devisers of the regulations, and the minds of authoritarians involved in other kinds of punitive institutions. The same principle was discernible in the Greenwich Village production by Fernando Arrabal of his own theatre-of-cruelty prison play *And They Put Handcuffs on the Flowers*: the real shocks in it came from the accounts of tortures and defilements that had actually occurred in Franco's prisons, and from the harangues by dignitaries in which one heard authentic Falangist or Spanish-clerical rhetoric about the Nation, Duty, Obedience, etc. The nudity and artificial blood, on the other hand, were wholly undisturbing; and the context made clear why. The initial shock-effect of nudity on stage in the 1960s came from the feeling that it was a bit disturbing to the actors themselves, and that in effect the director was perpetrating a violence upon them by compelling them to exhibit themselves, and the audience a kind of violation by looking at them. In other words, one was able temporarily to encounter a disturbed but focused mode of consciousness (even if only one's own) of a sort that could exist outside the confines of the theatre And insofar as this occurs, theatrical nudity can still be shocking. It would have been shocking, for example, to have felt in Arrabal's play that one was convincingly in the presence of a young and modest Republican woman naked among Falangists, like Djamila Bouhired naked among her torturers in Algiers.[10] As it was, however, there were simply good-looking actors gratuitously unclothed in front of a respectful audience.

And what happens with the shown violences of *The Brig*, or the narrated ones of *And They Put Handcuffs*, or those of *Macbeth*, or *King Lear*, or *Oedipus Rex* is what happens with most of the distinguished works that, whether literally violent or not, one thinks of automatically as violent and in some sense revolutionary. Despite all the formal abrasiveness, the expressive dislocations and heightenings, works like Céline's *Mort à crédit*, or Rimbaud's *Un saison en enfer*, or some of Van Gogh's St Remy paintings, or Goya's *Caprichios*, or Picasso's *Guernica* act as windows, and it is in relation to what one sees through them – bourgeois awfulness, or the horrors of war, or intensities of ecstasy or dread, and so on that the deepest challenges and confrontations occur.[11] If one is made to feel more or less deeply uncomfortable, it is because one is being confronted with facts that one hadn't known, or hadn't thought carefully enough about, or is still reluctant to feel intensely enough about. In 'Political Position of Today's Art' (1935), André Breton observes:

> We know that the adjective 'revolutionary' is generously applied to every work, to every intellectual creator who appears to break with tradition. I say 'appears to break', for that mysterious entity, tradition, that some attempt to describe as being very exclusive, has proved for centuries to have a boundless capacity for assimilation. This adjective, which hastily takes into account the indisputable nonconformist will that quickens such a work, such a creator, has the grave defect of being confused with one which tends to define a systematic action aiming at the transformation

of the world and implying the necessity of concretely attacking its real bases.[12]

The right kinds of violent works do indeed involve a concern with and, insofar as they are revolutionary in intention, an attempt to transform the 'real bases' of things. And it is because of that, and not because of any taboo-breaking or violation,[13] that some of them answer in some measure to Artaud's assertion that 'the action of ["cruel"] theatre, like that of plague, is beneficial, for, impelling men to see themselves as they are, it causes the mask to fall, reveals the lie, the slackness, baseness, and hypocrisy of our world. . . .' (p. 31).

But if physical violences in art can indeed shock one into a greater awareness in the same way that the plague in Oran shocked and challenged the protagonists in Camus' *La peste*, a prerequisite of their doing so in any consequential way is that they genuinely carry one out into the real world. And in that world, the primary fact about violence is that it hurts, that sometimes it hurts appallingly, and that one wouldn't want violences to be inflicted on oneself. It therefore becomes of considerable importance not to fall into confusion if one feels that violences, even the most extreme violences, can have very beneficial consequences in art. In the early 1950s, Warshow pointed out that the intellectuals' recoil from and disdain for violence had 'helped to free it from moral control by letting it take on the aura of "emancipation". The celebration of acts of violence is left more and more to the irresponsible. . .' (p. 103). There seems to me to be a contrary danger now of intellectuals themselves being irresponsible in their dealings with violence, especially in the arts.

As I have intimated, one route involves an attempt to intellectualize violences, to make them part of a system, to see them as part of an intellectual campaign against society. The other involves the attempt to reduce violence to an essentially non-intellectual mode of self-expression and self-affirmation, a way of escaping – or at least trying to escape – from the felt tyranny of intellectualization. Both seem to me to involve losing sight of, or blurring, those basic facts about violence that I mentioned above. And either way the consciousnesses of victims and victimizers gets falsified and the border between life and art is erased in the wrong way, namely by the reduction of life to the status of art – mostly not very good art. Where victimizers are concerned, 'Who's Who in the New Cult of Violence', as I have said, is very revealing in this way. As for victims, I have little doubt that for a sizeable number of people learning about it at second hand, the student sit-in at Columbia University in 1968 took on so much the air of a Happening or a Theatre-of-Cruelty performance that the policeman who, according to Diana Trilling, was paralysed for life by a student's jumping on him[14] became assimilated as a kind of stage-prop to the wastebasket in President Grayson Kirk's office into which a student urinated in a neo-Dada gesture. Either way, art suffers as well: the sought-for therapeutic shocks don't in fact occur, or else occur with diminishing force and frequency. And too easy an assent to the idea of violence – I mean, an assent that results from ignorance and sentimentality – is capable of leading insidiously to an overtenderness towards the kind of brutal 'realistic' violences that I have referred to, or towards more overtly Fascist attitudes.

What I shall chiefly be concerned with in the rest of this book, therefore, are realistic violences of a sort that one wishes *wouldn't* occur – violences of the sort that one encounters some of the time in the works of Shakespeare, Céline, Crane, Goya, Hemingway, Clouzot, Franju, and

Zola – violences that aren't fun at all. ('The Greeks were nice chaps too. When they evacuated they had all their baggage animals they couldn't take off with them so they just broke their forelegs and dumped them into the shallow water. All those mules with their forelegs broken pushed over into the shallow water. It was all a pleasant business. My word yes a most pleasant business.' Thus Hemingway in 'On the Quai at Smyrna'; and when he returned to the incident later in 'A Natural History of the Dead', he said appropriately that it would have taken a Goya to depict it.) What I shall be mainly concerned with are violences that may indeed occur in 'cruel' works or in works accompanied by a good deal of expressive intensifying and heightening, but that owe their effectiveness not primarily to the formal daring of the work but to the simple fact that one believes that such violences could actually happen. Ezra Pound has called literature 'news that STAYS news'.[15] I shall try to define some of the features of the kind of violence that stays disturbing however often one returns to it.

VICTIMS

Let me start with a couple of cruel jokes that form useful paradigms. The first is of a familiar American kind: 'Question: What is yellow and black and screams when it rolls over? Answer: A school bus.' The second is English and dates back at least twenty-five years. Scene: an English bus; characters, the driver behind his glass partition, a passenger on the seat just behind him, another passenger looking on. Man behind driver raps on partition, driver looks round, man waggles a piece of string at him and grins, driver glowers apoplectically and hunches over the wheel. After several repetitions, the spectator finally asks the obvious question. 'Oh,' says the string-wagger, 'e's got no sense of humour; 'is brother was 'anged this morning.'

Now, the first joke, as I said, is of a familiar kind, and a number of other examples would have done just as well: e.g., the Helen Keller doll – you wind it up and it bumps into the furniture; or, 'Mummy, Mummy, why can't I go out and play?' 'If I've told you once I've told you a thousand times. You've got leukemia'; or, 'But apart from that, Mrs Lincoln, how did you enjoy the play?' Jokes of this sort (which on first hearing are sometimes disturbingly funny) are essentially 'idea' jokes – jokes rather akin, in certain ways, to some of the movies of Godard or to a novel like Burroughs' *Naked Lunch*. They are nasty, of course, but that is their point. They are a form of counter-aggression. They affront all the

American liberal–suburbanizing pressures making for uniform, unrelaxed postures of Sympathy, Pity, Good Works, and so on – pressures, in other words, towards a bland, ego-suppressing, and essentially not-thought-through niceness – and they often make a valid point of sorts. I mean, if they are 'inhuman', the cliché-attitudes that they are going up against do themselves dehumanize people by reducing them all to types (the sick and maimed all martyrs, children all little loveable purities, the great suburban–liberal heroes all impossible paragons of nobility in a *Reader's Digest* way, etc.). However, they are only endurable because of the very mechanism that makes them funny, namely that the mind, directed at first towards real people or kinds of people, recognizes almost instantaneously that what is really under attack is certain other kinds of people *thinking* about them, and so veers away from a serious contemplation of the objects themselves. A de-realizing of the physical occurs in other kinds of humour too, of course, especially the Tom-and-Jerry kind and the Ruthless Rhymes kind. But in the former the protagonists' interminable, ballet-like pursuit and counter-pursuit, aggression and counter-aggression (in which nothing is irrevocable and the body is indestructible) are simply an expressive heightening of the deadpan trading of insults between friends who know each other's deeper attitudes so well that they can afford to be abominably rude to each other. (*The Importance of Being Earnest* comes to mind here too, as do certain kinds of clown acts and comedy teams.) And in Ruthless Rhymes like 'Eating more than he was able,/John fell dead at the breakfast table./"Mummy dear," said sister Meg,/"May I have Johnny's other egg?",'[1] the plots are impossible, the callousness presented as such, and the pleasures those of a tidied-up and harmless fantasy so outrageous that there is no possibility of confusing it with actuality. The de-realizations involved here, in other words, are of the sort that enables one to withdraw temporarily, with a clear conscience, from the complexities of human behaviour and from certain kinds of ethical claims.

In the second of the two bus jokes, in contrast, there is neither de-realization nor escape, and the more one goes on filling in the human realities of the three characters, the weightier the joke becomes. One has, I mean, the trapped rage of the driver who is dutifully Doing His Job and allowing the other man to remain inviolable behind his magic badge of Member of the Public, and the devastating unwitting self-exposure of the joke-maker to a neutral observer; and with that self-exposure comes an agreeably tart subverting of the English over-exaltation of the value of a sense of humour. Even though the action may be a distasteful one, the representative attitudes and relationships of the three men are more lasting than the shadowy cliché-liberal opponent implicit in the school-bus joke, and I suspect that the latter and other jokes like it will shrivel up and blow away as soon as its antagonists have gone. The second bus, however, can go chugging along for ever in the mind through Clapham or Willesden or wherever it is, and it will continue to carry a very solid cargo of Englishness – and not just of Englishness but of the three essential figures of the violated, the violater, and the more or less decent spectator.

I suggest that this joke is paradigmatic of the most meaningful – and, as I shall explain further on, most daring – kind of violence in certain important ways. It involves a penetration into and empathy with other consciousnesses in action. The value-systems of those involved both differ from each other markedly and are thoroughly embodied in and expressed through the movements of the flesh. The attitudes of the narrator too are substantially embodied in and revealed through the physical action. And the narrator's 'cruelty' towards his audience consists in compelling them to look, with him, at certain disquieting human possibilities. I shall consider first the question of empathy, and shall confine myself in this chapter to the question of empathy with victims. What makes the question important and problematic, it seems to me, is the ease with which empathy *doesn't* occur.

A failure of empathy is not necessarily bad. It is obvious that not only in jokes but in a good many other works of entertainment, like children's Westerns, sword-play costume dramas of the Douglas Fairbanks kind, Italian Hercules movies, and a host of animated cartoons, one is dealing just as much with 'As If' worlds as one is in *Alice in Wonderland* – worlds which in some ways overlap the physical one that we inhabit, but in others differ from it sharply. And this is worth bearing in mind where the question of censorship is concerned, above all with respect to the works of Sade. There are varying degrees of reality in Sade, of course, and some of the descriptions by the former whorehouse madams in *Les cent vingt jours de Sodome* vibrate with actuality. Yes, one feels, this or that particular act, in its grotesquerie and squalor, is exactly the sort of thing that one could have expected to find in an expensive brothel during the *Ancien régime*. But it is important to note a curious paradox about the other parts of that unpleasant work, and about *Juliette* and *Les infortunes de la vertu* and *La nouvelle Justine*. At first sight, a fictional statement like 'They require a woman whose pregnancy is in its eighth or has begun its ninth month, they open her belly, snatch out the child, burn it before the mother's eyes, and in its place substitute a package containing sulphur . . ., which they set afire, then stitch the belly up again, leaving the mother thus to perish in the midst of incredible agonies, while they look on . . .' is almost as dreadful as a factual one like 'The widow of one . . . police captain was forced to look on in horror as the [rebels] beheaded her children, disemboweled her husband and stuffed the children's heads into his stomach. Then she was raped repeatedly and left for dead.'[2] But the dreadfulness of Sade's note comes substantially from its being detached from its context, so that the reader perforce locates the action in the world as he himself knows it. A crucial difference of Sade's world, however, is that it is almost impossible to empathize with the victims in it. The victims in the half-a-million or so words of *Juliette*, for example, run into the thousands, perhaps even the tens of thousands, but out of all of them I can bring to mind only two or three instances that in their contexts are genuinely shocking. But it seems to me precisely this that helps to substantiate the distinction continually made by French intellectuals between the Sadean and the sadistic, and to support the contention that Sade was not sadistic in the conventional sense of the word, and that reading him in bulk – as distinct from reading him in excerpts or in bowdlerized versions – does not offer the gratifications that are furnished by vastly inferior sado-masochistic works, or by something like Octave Mirbeau's *Le jardin des supplices*.[3] As more than one critic has pointed out, an obvious factor in the constant escalation of each of Sade's main works – an escalation in the magnitude of the cruelties and crimes, and even more an escalation in the numbers of the victims – is that at virtually no point in the relationships between the victim and the violator is the victim real in the way that produces the warm quasi-sexual thrill obtaining, I take it, in a good many conventionally sadistic situations, whether the beating of school-boys, or the torture-killings by someone like Neville

Heath, or some of the interrogations of 'witches' during the heyday of the Inquisition in Germany, or the fictional raping and torturing described in Selby's *The Room*.

But while one can and does respond more or less numbly to a good many situations and characters in all kinds of fiction, a numbness of response is both more obvious where violent than where non-violent works are concerned, and, sometimes, more disturbing. In ordinary novels and short stories it is usually perfectly satisfactory to give to the bulk of the characters only the surface reality that is necessary for them to impinge on the protagonists. Normally no intense immediate sympathy with them is needed, and sympathy can often be withheld entirely when they are presented as more or less villainous in their relationship to hero or heroine. Where violences are involved, however, each victim of it becomes momentarily a sort of hero himself, in that behind the surface a good deal of intense feeling must be presumed to be going on that underlines not his differences from the reader but his kinship. And accordingly a novelist – or for that matter any kind of artist – offering to deal in violences has to work unusually hard at achieving immediacy of response. We can accept on trust the reality of Jane Austen's Mr Collins without in the least caring how it would feel to be Mr Collins at this or that moment. But we have all known acute pain at one time or another, and we know immediately when we are failing to get the 'pain' experience in a fictional situation where someone is suffering more or less acutely. What, then, produces the empathy? What produces the sense of shock or horror or (when violences are imminent rather than actually happening) fear that is a common denominator alike in children being disturbed by television violences and adults watching *King Lear*.

To begin with, it obviously helps in a general way

where there are the fewest accretions of distance, foreign-
ness, and sheer 'otherness' that need transposing into
terms of one's own experience. In Flaubert's *Salammbô*,
for instance, the four most shocking passages are the
accounts of the valley of crucified lions, of the pathetic-
ally mutilated elephants in Hamilcar's palace, of the
galled and ravenous slaves toiling at the mill there, and
of the slow tearing to death of the Libyan leader Matho
as he is compelled to walk the gauntlet between the rows
of enraged citizens in Carthage; and the first two seem
to me decidedly the more immediate in their impact. For
example,

> C'était un lion, attaché à une croix par les quatre
> membres comme un criminal. Son mufle énorme lui
> retombait sur la poitrine, et ses deux pattes antérieures,
> disparaissant à demi sous l'abondance de sa crinière,
> étaient largement écartées comme les deux ailes d'un
> oiseau. Ses côtes, une à une, saillissaient sous sa peau
> tendue; ses jambes de derrière, clouées l'une contre
> l'autre, remontaient un peu; et du sang noir, coulant
> parmi ses poils, avait amassé des stalactites au bas de
> sa queue qui pendait toute droite le long de la croix.[4]

Orwell took cognizance of this kind of paradox in
'Marrakech', in his examination of the ease with which
on a visit to Morocco in the 1930s, he himself could feel
rage at the sufferings of overburdened donkeys while
almost literally not seeing the little old women shuffling
along under enormous bundles of firewood.[5] And in the
earlier 'Shooting an Elephant', it is plain that not only
for the Orwell of the Imperial Police but for the Orwell
writing the reminiscence, the elephant is in some ways
more real, more *sympathique*, more human even, than
the crowd of Burmese rejoicing at the prospect of its

death. Partly, no doubt, what is involved is our instinctive recognition of the innocence of animals, even predatory wild ones, of their defencelessness when domesticated, of the absence in them of ideology and articulate intention, of the meaninglessness of the notion of 'punishing' lions or elephants, and of the particular nastiness at times of the enjoyment of inflicting pain on them. Hence a single sentence in the Bricksville section of *Huckleberry Finn* apropos of the loafers in the run-down Arkansas town is in some ways more coldly horrible than the whole brilliant and shocking account there of the gunning down of the drunken old man, Boggs, by the local aristocrat, Colonel Sherburn: 'There couldn't anything wake them up all over, and make them happy all over, like a dog-fight – unless it might be putting turpentine on a stray dog and setting fire to him, or tying a tin pan to his tail and see him run himself to death' (ch. 21). But I think that the lack of alienating accretions that I spoke of is even more important and that the effect of such accretions needs to be taken into account by those who abominate their consequences.

It is not surprising that for so many Americans the My Lai massacre was self-evidently not in the same class as the Nazi massacres of civilians at Lidice or Oradour. And probably most readers of Paul Bowles' *The Delicate Prey* must have been upset a good deal more by the story in which an imprudent professor is kidnapped by a desert band and, his tongue having been cut out, is used as a money-making clown, than by the story in which an Arab, after sexually mutilating in an atrocious fashion another Arab whom he has captured, violates him and next morning saws through his windpipe with an old razor, being subsequently repaid by being buried up to his neck in the desert sand and left to bake to death. What makes a person of a different colour appear alien, when he or she *does* appear alien, is not simply the colour itself or the configuration of the features, but the difficulty that one has in decoding the finer signals of facial expressions and bodily gestures. The same kind of difficulty arises in a particularly poignant form in the case of individuals of one's own culture whose faces have been hideously mutilated in war or in civil accidents; the very thing that cries out for the deepest sympathy serves in some measure to inhibit that sympathy, namely the conversion of the sufferers into 'monsters'.[6] And related to both is the fact that an immediate, an intuitive sympathy only occurs when one believes that one knows with reasonable precision how the victim is himself perceiving and judging what is happening to him. Sympathy with the alien is usually something that has to be *learned*. And I suspect that some of the more odious reported cruelties and callousnesses of American troops in Vietnam may have occurred because of the frustration that builds up when someone is uneasily aware both that he ought to be feeling sympathy and that in fact he doesn't feel it or even feels irritation or hostility, so that in self-defence against the accumulating sense of guilt he converts the cause of it into an object that doesn't deserve any sympathy – a conversion that is easiest to effect by doing violences to it.

It seems likely, furthermore, that similar reactions occur among television-viewers and movie-goers and that they are the more likely to occur as superficial documentary information about alien cultures multiplies. The trouble with second- or third-rate 'serious' artists is that they provide enough information to emphasize the *differentness* of the people or peoples that they are talking about or filming (unlike, say, the Sheik or Sarong kind of Hollywood movie in which one is patently never out of Southern California) but not enough to make the breakthrough into real empathy possible. This problem of alienness and of the interrelationship between sympathy, empathy, understanding, and knowledge has also come up where the concentration camps are concerned. As has been testified to again and again, one of the strongest feelings of *concentrationnaires* after their release was the seeming impossibility of conveying to outsiders what the experience was like,[7] and related to this, almost certainly, was the implicit recognition that by endeavouring to do so they were in fact estranging themselves from their listeners and converting themselves into a species of freaks or monsters. There seems to me a good deal of wisdom to Yeats' remark that 'passive suffering is not a theme for tragedy'.[8] In general, passivity does not invite empathy. What does invite it – what enables one to project oneself into someone else's world and see it as continuous with the one that one knows oneself – is anything that permits one to see the other as an agent. Animals, especially domestic animals, and very young children are perceptibly agents all the time, engaged continuously in the business of living, and without any conceptual apparatus that organizes their aspirations and fear in complex unfamiliar ways. Where more highly structured psyches are concerned, two of the most important factors making for empathy are a sense of the individual as engaged in work, and a sense of the physicality of the body. The first is the simpler of the two.

In a documentary made in North Vietnam two or three years ago, a mutilated and bandaged young boy was shown in hospital, and it was explained that he had been out in the fields with the family buffalo when the American machine-gunners passed overhead. At the end of this brief section the narrator added, as if it were an afterthought, that the buffalo had been killed, and I imagine that I was not the only member of the audience to have been jolted thereby into a fuller sympathy with the boy. Obviously the information was not an afterthought at all but the result of an intelligent recognition of the kind of difficulties that I have been speaking of. For the point was not merely that another innocent being had been wantonly struck down. It was also that the sensed loss of that gentle and valuable animal for both the boy and the family enabled one suddenly to penetrate much more deeply into the working daily world of those people. To penetrate into a person's work or the work of a group is in a real sense to penetrate into the person or group too. A major breakthrough in the history of the presentation of labouring-class people in England, for example, came around the turn of the century when George Sturt got beyond the surface differentiae of labourers and did for them what Kipling had so influentially done for the common soldiers, service–middle-class administrators, and young subalterns in India. Hence the success and importance of what can be called the domestic accounts of concentration camp life. More, even, than so distinguished a work as Eugen Kogon's *Theory and Practice of Hell*, works like David Rousset's *L'Univers concentrationnaire*, Viktor E. Frankl's *From Death Camp to Existentialism*, Primo Levi's *Si questo è un uomo*, Bruno Bettelheim's *The Informed Heart*, and Tadeusz Borowski's *This Way for the Gas, Ladies and Gentlemen*[9] enable one to grasp what it would be like to be in a camp oneself during an ordinary working day, with the entailed hopes, fears, anxieties, and stratagems for enduring the unendurable. Hence too the wide appeal of Alexander Solzhenitsyn's *One Day in the Life of Ivan Denisovich*, and the more restricted esteem accorded such low-keyed prison movies as Bresson's *Un condamné à mort est échappé* and Becker's *Le trou.*

And the same holds true of other kinds of works, too. One of the factors responsible for the lack of sympathy with the victims in a good many horror movies is that, as in *Les cent vingt jours de Sodome* and substantial parts of *Justine* and *Juliette*, there is either an almost literally closed-off situation – a castle, an old dark house, an island – from which there is no escape and in which the victims, having been brought there by chance or force or trickery, can engage in almost none of the kinds of workaday activities that could give us a sense of them existing as normal social beings with social roles to play; or else the setting is Transylvania or the fogs of Victorian London, with again a very restricted range of workaday stimuli and responses permitted to the characters. (The murdered girls, if they work at all, are almost invariably implausible serving wenches or equally implausible prostitutes.) And, contrariwise, a good part of the humanity and moral delicacy of Browning's *Freaks* derives from the fact that the actual circus freaks who constitute most of the cast are presented not as monsters but as working men and women engaged, poignantly, in the daily business of collaboratively earning their living. Much the same principle seems to hold where the villains of horror movies and thrillers are concerned. In two of the most distinguished horror movies – *Les yeux sans visage* and *Peeping Tom* – Franju's Dr Genessier holds down a perfectly respectable job in modern Paris, as does Powell's compulsively murdering cameraman in a masterly evoked modern London. The general superiority of the Frankenstein movies to the Dracula ones, and their lesser vulnerability to irony and parody, are obviously partly due to the fact that Baron Frankenstein likewise has a social–professional role of a sort that is impossible to Count Dracula. And if thrillers like John McPartland's *Face of Evil* and Stanley Ellin's *The Eighth Circle* are a good deal more disquieting than one like Hammett's *Red Harvest* (his masterpiece, and essentially a *comic* novel, I believe), it is partly because the action in the latter is confined almost wholly to the sharply individuated criminal fraternity of an isolated small American city, who are engaged in conventional criminal activities, and who by the end have largely wiped each other out. In the first two, in contrast, one has the sense of glimpsing the edges of large and all-too-credible power systems in which organized crime, political corruption, and ruthless corporate business interlock.

The question of physicality, as I said, seems to me more complicated, and I find it more interesting. Let me turn again to 'entertainments' (in Graham Greene's sense of the term) to clarify what I mean.

In a culture as starved of physicality as ours, the enduring appeal of a good many violent works is not just that they are violent but that they re-immerse us vicariously in physical action. The best thrillers of writers like Hammett, Hamilton, Adam Hall, John D. MacDonald, Charles Williams, Ted Lewis, Peter O'Donnell, and Geoffrey Household, for example, give one a bracing awareness of what it feels like to engage in a variety of physical actions demanding great concentration, speed, and stamina. So do some of the best violent movies, such as Hodges' *Get Carter*, Kurosawa's *Seven Samurai*, and numerous Westerns. Much of Zinneman's *High Noon*, for instance, may have been *Kitsch*, but the final showdown wasn't, and one felt unforgettably what it was like to be an ageing man running and dodging through the dust and heat, straining to out-think and out-perform the murderous quartet who were hunting him, the body's impulses often virtually preceding those of the mind. The actions can also be less combative ones, like the various strenuous journeyings that figure in numerous other Westerns[10] and in some of the best thrillers of writers such as Simon Harvester, Arthur Upfield, Eric Ambler, John Welcome, Martin Woodhouse, and the prototypical Erskine Childers and John Buchan. But they too put one convincingly back in touch with a simpler world of the heroic body, a world not hopelessly remote from that of the Homeric epics and the Icelandic Sagas. Indeed, they may even do so more convincingly than most accounts of real-life adventurings.

And conversely, some of the most exasperating thrillers are those in which, as in Ian Flemming's, the author has offered to deal with violent action and is obviously faking. One of the most fundamental criticisms to be made of the Bond books, next to the feebleness of their plotting, is that the only strenuously muscular activities in them that are felt from the inside are those, such as skin-diving and judo, that are available to the ordinary desk-man on vacation or working out in the gym. Bond himself as an allegedly highly trained and ruthlessly functioning fighting body is simply a hole in the air when compared, say, with Hamilton's Matt Helm, or O'Donnell's Willy Garvin, or Lewis's Jack Carter. No doubt it is this fact, and the even greater feebleness displayed in the movies, that helps to account for the Bond boom, since it is reassuring for the ordinary reader to see a hero who may be handsomer but isn't disturbingly more physically competent than he is himself. But the authorial fakings and fumblings are exasperating in themselves, and since the villains similarly lack muscularity (consider, for example, the ludicrous stomping with football boots in *Diamonds are Forever*) the nastier violences wear all the more the look of authorial contrivance and calculation rather than of being natural by-products of the activities of convincingly violent men. A similar fumbling can of course go on in more respectable works too, such as G. K.

64

Chesterton's *The Napoleon of Notting Hill*. Prose like 'Then men ducked instinctively at the rushing noise of the sword coming down out of the sky, and Wilson of Bayswater was smashed and wiped down upon the floor like a fly. Nothing was left of him but a wreck . . .' (book IV, ch. 3), which is almost literally the sort of thing one finds in some of the current violent comic books, is the prose of someone who simply does not know what he is talking about.

But the truth is that in the majority of violent entertainments the body as a complex tissue of sensitivities and fatigues, an organism with its own insistent rules and reactions, is really no more sharply present than it is in most erotica. And the really deplorable thing about most of the violences adduced so indignantly in works like Legman's *Love and Death* and Wertham's *A Sign for Cain* is that physically they aren't violent enough. The physical imperviousness of private eyes to sappings, beatings-up, knees in the groin, and so on, is a commonplace by now, and at times is obviously done tongue-in-cheek. (In the Shell Scott books of Richard S. Prather, for example, one is simply in Woody Woodpecker country.) The bar-room fight in Huston's *Treasure of the Sierre Madre* is close to being unique in its acknowledgment of the sheer exhaustion brought about in an all-out fist-fight, almost independently of the damage done by the blows themselves. In only three or four out of literally hundreds of thrillers have I found it acknowledged that sudden death and acute fear can cause a relaxation of the sphincter muscles, all of them, as I recall, being by John D. MacDonald. Household's *Rogue Male* is virtually the only thriller in which it is acknowledged that even a hero's body defecates. The corpse of the plainclothesman shot by accident at the very end of Friedkin's *The French Connection* is almost the only one I can recall seeing in a movie which gave one a sharp sense of the *difference* of a dead body – of the sense of something emptied, discarded, thrown away; and in virtually no movies of any kind is the bloating of corpses shown, which contributes to the faint air of implausibility of even as good a war movie as Kubrick's *Paths of Glory*. Again, in very few thrillers are the long-term physical-psychological consequences of having been severely tortured or methodically beaten up acknowledged convincingly, as they are in Conrad's *Nostromo*: MacDonald's *Death Trap* and *The Executioners* (*Cape Fear*), Household's *Rogue Male*, McPartland's *Face of Evil*, and Hamilton's *Date with Darkness* and *The Steel Mirror* are the only ones that I can bring to mind, though no doubt there are a handful of others. And altogether there are extremely few entertainments that are violent in truly shocking ways – shocking, I mean, as Watkin's *Culloden*, or Franju's *Le sang des bêtes*, or Selby's *The Room*, or the shotgun suicide in Céline's *Mort à crédit*, or the blinding of Gloucester in *Lear* are shocking. One almost never has to avert one's eyes from the screen or make an effort not to lay down the book; rather, one waits with fascination for what is coming next, and one *is* entertained. Hence, of course, the rage induced in English reviewers by Franju's *Les yeux sans visage* when it was first shown; here was a horror movie that actually dared to be horrifying.[11] For all their violences, violent entertainments normally involve a blanking out of the really unpleasant, and tend to promote a sense of security and invulnerability in the reader or viewer. I wish to suggest that a very important way in which certain violences shock us – and shock salutarily – is that they undermine the yearning for invulnerability that violent entertainments cater to.

At its crudest, such a yearning is gratified by simply

refraining from considering certain possibilities. The movie-goer, or television-watcher, or thriller-reader can give himself up to dreams of violent glory in a way that invites the tart comment in John D. MacDonald's *One Fearful Yellow Eye* that 'the gutsy dramas on the mass media tend to make us forget that the average urban male is so unaccustomed to sudden pain that if you mash his nose flat, he'll be nauseated for hours, spend two days in bed, and be shaky for the rest of the week' (ch. 7). The author of *Histoire d'O* can prudently ignore the question of what it would be like being ravished while one had a bad headache, or a cold, or haemorrhoids, or cystitis. Maurice Blanchot can advance with seeming approval Sade's belief that the right kind of people can convert anything into pleasure: it would be interesting to see how they would cope with the castor-oil treatment of the Fascist *squadristi*, let alone with the more bestial concentration camp torments. And one could go on multiplying examples indicative of a craving for changes in the rules of violence that would help to make engaging in violences oneself, at least in imagination, a pleasurably penalty-free matter, Sade himself being the supreme exemplar of such a craving. In part all this, particularly nowadays, is a manifestation of a general desire not to be reminded of disturbing possibilities inhering in the body. It is noteworthy, for instance, how automobile accidents in our culture are presented almost wholly in terms of death – so tidily dramatic and final and conventionally tragic – rather than in terms of broken septums, damaged sinuses, smashed teeth, amputations, months of bed-ridden pain and discomfort, blindness, facial scars, and so on. And I was not the only newspaper reader, I imagine, to have been less shocked by accounts of the deaths resulting from the bombings in Northern Ireland than by an account, partly in their own words, of the continuing physical sufferings of some of the girl operators who had been injured in the bombing of a telephone exchange and had since returned to work

An impatience with the Romantic retreat from the physical, including Sade's own, was partly responsible, I take it, for such salutary reminders as the far from aesthetic visit of Des Esseintes to the tooth-puller in J.-K. Huysmans' *À rebours*, or Artaud's magnificent description in *Le théâtre et son double* of the processes going on in a plague-infected body, or Camus' use of the plague in *La peste*, or the account in *Mort à crédit* of the death of Dr Gustin, especially this: 'In the end he died of a heart attack, under circumstances that were anything but cozy. An attack of angina pectoris that lasted twenty minutes. He held out for a hundred and twenty seconds with his classical memories, his resolutions, the example of Caesar . . . But for eighteen minutes he screamed like a stuck pig . . .'[12] But then in a sense Céline's whole book is the work of someone in revolt against traditional French romanticism and compelled to submit his own Sadean aspirations, his cravings for power and plenitude, to the test of the everyday, including the claims of the body and the necessity to earn one's living. That this kind of drawing attention to the unaesthetic aspects of the body feels different from the way in which it often occurs in American literature – e.g., in the account of the 'huge seagull, busily gorging itself' on the putrescent corpse in Poe's *Narrative of Arthur Gordon Pym* (ch. 10), or the image of the wild hogs eating wounded men in Ambrose Bierce's 'Coup de Grace', or Hemingway's reference in 'A Natural History of the Dead' to corpses 'in the hot weather with a half-pint of maggots working where their mouths have been' – is partly attributable, I suppose, to the fact that in French literature an awareness of the inescapability of the body goes back at least to Rabelais and the Villon of 'Frères humains, qui après nous vivez.' The body has been suspect much of the time in American literature, perhaps because it is the body that most ineluctably sets limits to individual human ambitions, however sublime or generous.

However, a catering to one's yearnings for invulnerability or inviolability can occur in more complex ways. Works involving violences, like other kinds, tend to accumulate their conventions and to fall into certain patterns. And if one is out for relaxation, one can hardly have too many conventional elements, especially in horror movies and Westerns – the heroine's panic-stricken flight through a midnight forest as Something makes ominous noises in the underbrush alongside the path; the rifle barrel easing out of an upper-storey hotel window as the hero rides up the main street; and so on. But the relaxation – the fundamental relaxation as distinct from a pleasurable tension and tingling in part of one's mind – is possible only because of certain implicit limits. The Something doesn't catch up with the heroine, the rifle speaks but the hero doesn't fall dead; and in both cases the experienced viewer is not surprised. Of course there are ostensible variations, and it may sometimes not be easy to explain to a less experienced viewer why it is 'right' for one particular hero in a *two*-hero Western to be killed in the last reel, or for one particular starlet to be chewed up by the werewolf, but not for another. But in general the limits are fairly clearly marked: there are individuals to whom violences of certain kinds are simply not going to happen, and others to whom they may and who in a sense are expendable.

The appeal of the indestructibility of a good many heroes is obvious enough; it is partly what has made the *Odyssey* so perennially enjoyable. It is always enjoyable to be able to identify with someone who is skilful, clever, and above all lucky, especially when the skills displayed by him are indeed convincing (as with Hammett's Continental Op, and Modesty Blaise and Willy Garvin, and several of the *samurai* played by Toshiro Mifune) and sometimes even when they are preposterous (as in Leone's 'Dollar' Westerns, and Chinese 'sword' movies, and Douglas Fairbanks' costume adventures). This kind of invulnerability is generally vicious only insofar as a seriously-intended crusading element is involved, by which I mean that one is invited to identify oneself self-righteously with the hero as he punishes dehumanized villains who *deserve* to suffer and for whom one needn't feel the least flicker of sympathy – 'outlaw[s] against whom anything is permissible', as Orwell put it in 'Raffles and Miss Blandish'.[13] The crusading punishment of odious or contemptible but in any case slightly unreal villains is a common denominator not only in the Bond books, the early Mike Hammer books, and the like, but also in episodes such as the war in Heaven in *Paradise Lost* and the activities of Artegall and his robotic servant Talus in Book V of *The Faerie Queene*. Contrariwise, some of the more memorable moments in fiction are those in which fearsome villains suddenly become humanized at the point at which they themselves, usually quite justly, become victims. The most striking instance of this is probably that in which the blinded Cyclops tenderly addresses his favourite ram, under which Odysseus is hiding; another is that at the end of *Oliver Twist* in which, after the hunted Bill Sykes has fallen to his death at the end of the rope attached to the chimney stack, his still-faithful dog leaps after him; and there are two or three memorable instances in the Mexican novels of B. Traven, especially *The Treasure of the Sierra Madre* and *General from the Jungle*. However, it is a different kind

70

of invulnerability and a different species of victim that interests me most here.

The expendable figures in movies are in a sense almost always 'natural' victims, so that the violences are in some way felt to be appropriate. The most obvious appropriateness, in terms of plot, is when the people involved are all professionally violent men who know the risks they are running – gladiators, gunfighters, professional criminals, and the like. A prize-fight is one of the most obvious real-life examples of this, and it is significant that almost no deeply moving films have been made about the fight business. Wise's *The Set-Up* has stayed in my mind, but it is years since I saw it, and perhaps it hasn't worn well; as for Visconti's *Rocco and His Brothers*, the truly moving parts, as I recall, were all extraneous to the actual fighting. (I have not, at the time of writing, been able to see Huston's *Fat City*.) But even non-violent victims in a lot of movies take risks that *invite* violences – the over-sanguine homesteaders in Indian territory, for example, or the pea-brained blonde who inevitably goes prospecting in the cellars of the castle where she is spending the night, quite as if she herself had never seen a horror movie in her life. And naturally the violences arrive on cue, in a sort of symbiotic relationship between victims and violators in which one is often emotionally on the side of the violator or would-be violator, whatever the surface ethics of the situation may be. A good deal of frustration can be induced, for instance, by the sort of nice girl (Mia Farrow in *Rosemary's Baby* is a prime specimen, but there are plenty of others in the type of thriller that at least one publishing house classifies on the dust-jacket as 'Damsel in Distress') who is plainly acting, in an inversion of the invulnerability of some heroes, with a lack of gumption so markedly *below* what one hopes one might be capable of oneself that one instinctively resists being drawn into sympathy and approval because of the temporary lessening of one's own vitality that would be entailed therein.

And frustration with what might be called the Clarissa type of behaviour – the supreme expression of which frustration is Sade's *Justine* – can also occur insidiously at times when reading or hearing about real-life victims. The bafflement induced in a good many Israeli *sabras* by the accounts of European Jewish communities going un-protestingly to their deaths is well-known. I suspect, too, that one of the reasons why it is possible to read through a book like Guy Chapman's thick anthology of selections from first-hand accounts of the First World War[14] with-out feeling any sharp sense of the awfulness of being a conscript in that war is that one receives no sense of those involved struggling against or even especially resenting their conditions. And one of the things to keep in mind about the poor and the unemployed is that the forces that demoralize them thereby also diminish sympathy for them by making them seem in some measure natural victims or 'losers'. Which is why almost any show of violence on their part, any collective demon-stration of spirit and protest, however ill-coordinated and 'illogical', is preferable to quiescence.

But while a number of victims in works of entertain-ment are natural ones, there are also, as I have said, a number of people whom one normally doesn't expect to become victims at all, and hence a number of violences that are likely to seem eminently unnatural. Gentle old priests, loving mothers, happy newly-weds, innocent children, and so on – the list can be considerably extended, and of course it is in some ways a cliché list, which is why people have been so grateful for a figure like W. C. Fields and remarks like 'Anyone who hates children and dogs can't be all bad,' and why too a horror

movie like Romero's *Night of the Living Dead* is so refreshing a change from the normal run of beleaguered-
fortress movies. Grand Guignol theatre, of which the
most distinguished specimen is probably André de
Lorde's *Les infernels*,[15] obviously owed a sizeable part of
its appeal to its reversal of conventional theatrical patterns
of inviolability. (Which is to say that the fundamental
objection to it was not that it was bloody but that it was
essentially parasitic.) But while some violations of taboos
are enjoyable or at least understandable, others are not.
No one who saw De Mille's *The Plainsman* as a child in
the 1930s, I imagine, has ever really got over the shock of
Gary Cooper's being casually shot in the back at the end
of it. And an important element in that shock was obviously the feeling that by his exemplary conduct in the
movie he had earned the right not to have that sort of
thing happen to him. Similarly a good part of the tension
of *The Most Dangerous Game* comes from what may be
called the double-jeopardy effect in it; the hero and
heroine have earned their right to live by escaping from
the shipwreck in shark-infested seas, only to be compelled to earn it all over again in the terms laid down by
the man-hunting Count Zaroff.

But I think that what is almost more likely to make for
a sense of unfairness is when a victim is trying to do
something that one feels he is entitled to finish doing. It
may be something dramatic, as in the kind of movie in
which the hero or heroine is shot just as he or she is
about to cross the frontier into freedom. It may be something very ordinary, as in Maupassant's 'Deux amis',
such as enjoying a quiet day's fishing in the country; or
something smaller still, as in the gratuitous shooting down
of the cowboy in Altman's *McCabe and Mrs. Miller* who
is trying to cross the little suspension bridge over the
frozen pond or stream in search of a pair of socks. It

may be a mixture of both, as in the murder of Janet Leigh in Hitchcock's *Psycho*, who has not only just resolved to purge herself of her offence and return the stolen money to her boss, but is now literally cleansing herself in the motel shower-bath after the day's tensions and fatigues. It may be a kind of dogged carrying-on, as in the case of the wife who, having managed to continue eking out a living in the bandit-swarming countryside of Mizoguchi's *Ugetsu Monagatari*, is casually killed towards the end of the movie. But what gets challenged in all such instances is what the great majority of violent works of entertainment reassuringly cater to, namely our feeling that when we ourselves are engaged in some reasonably natural and, in our own eyes at least, respectable activity, we too deserve to be allowed to bring it to a successful conclusion. Hence our sudden spurt of empathy, of indignation, sometimes even of fear when that assumption is challenged. A gap has suddenly closed; there is no longer on the one hand the normal and natural world that we ourselves inhabit and in which we are safe, and on the other a variety of more or less picturesque worlds in which violences happen merely to other people. And there is something else that often contributes to the closing of that gap.

Again and again in successful presentations of violence one's eye is caught by what French movie critics refer to as *l'insolite* – the unusual, the odd, the incongruous detail or constellation of details, the unexpected conjunction. The most brilliant account of modern battle I know is *The Red Badge of Courage*, for example, and it is brilliant precisely because the breakdown of stereotypes is one of its central preoccupations and because the details of battle that don't accord with its youthful hero's preconceptions have the vividness that is missing in Chapman's anthology and is only occasionally present even in Henri Barbusse's *Le feu.* 'Another [man] grunted suddenly as if he had been struck by a club in the stomach. He sat down and gazed ruefully. In his eyes there was mute, indefinite reproach. Farther up the line a man, standing behind a tree, had had his knee joint splintered by a ball. Immediately he had dropped his rifle and gripped the tree with both arms. And there he remained, clinging desperately and crying for assistance. . . .' (ch. 5) – that is the sort of thing in Crane's masterpiece that I mean. And this same kind of oddness distinguishes such episodes elsewhere as the rightly famous account of Fabrice's first coming under fire in Stendhal's *La chartreuse de Parme,* or the linking passages in Hemingway's *In Our Time,* or the final hand-to-hand combat of Modred and Arthur in Malory, or Grettir, in conversation with the berserker in the Grettir Saga, suddenly kicking up the bottom of the latter's shield while he is biting the upper rim of it in his rage, or Isaac Rosenberg's 'Break of Day in the Trenches', or a good many of the details of hand-to-hand combat in *The Iliad,* such as:

> . . . Patroklos coming close up to him stabbed with a
>   spear-thrust
> at the right side of the jaw and drove it on through the
>   teeth, then
> hooked and dragged him with the spear over the rail,
>   as a fisherman
> who sits out on the jut of a rock with a line and
>   glittering
> bronze hook drags a fish, who is thus doomed, out of
>   the water,
> so he hauled him, mouth open to the bright spear, out
>   of the chariot.[16]

Where less heroic violences are concerned, the unexpected is also to be found in a number of the best thrillers, such as the following all-too-kinaesthetic passage from the torture episode in Kenneth Millar's *Blue City*:

I was at the window before the scream ended, careless about whether I'd be seen or not. . . .

Joe Sault was in a kitchen chair half-facing me, with Kerch in front of him and Rusty behind him holding his arms. His left ear hung down like a red rag, dripping blood rhythmically onto his stylish collar. His mouth was ragged and spongy. His body was naked from the waist down, and his shirt had been rolled up under his armpits. His lean belly, bisected by a line of dark hair, trembled steadily like a beaten dog's.

Floraine was sitting with her fur-coated back to me, almost against the window. She didn't move and she didn't say a word. Garland was standing beside her, but all I could see of him was the grey elbow of his coat. The vibrating white light of a gasoline lamp on the table gave the room an ugliness as precise as a raw photograph.

Kerch put down the heavy iron spoon that he had been balancing in his hand, and picked up a paring-knife from the table. Before he began to move, I sensed that he was going to turn, and ducked. (ch. 13.)

And there is a common denominator to these and a number of other instances of *l'insolite* that serves to set them apart, as it does Villon's 'Frères humains . . .', from the grotesquerie of writers like Bierce and Poe. Again and again in the violences that permanently shock and disturb, one is made aware of the continuation of normal, non-violent life at the moment when the violences are occurring. And the relationship is usually a good deal less picturesque than that described by Auden in 'Musée des Beaux Arts', where 'the torturer's horse/ Scratches its innocent behind on a tree'. Kitchen utensils, domestic animals, trees, the corncob in Faulkner's *Sanctuary* (especially in the dreadful statement by one of the lynchers of the innocent Godwin, 'Only we never used a cob. We made him wish we had used a cob' [ch. 24]), the greenhouse and garden in which the torturing is done in Pabst's *Der Prozess*, the 'vile jelly' on which Cornwall sets his foot in *Lear*, the 'organic' comparisons in the death scenes in *Antony and Cleopatra*, the watering-trough in the woods in which the protagonist of *A Clockwork Orange* is held down and beaten, the reference in Walter Raleigh's 'Three things there be . . .' to the hemp 'which strings the hangman's bag', the laboratory animals and doves at the end of *Les yeux sans visage* – what results in such instances is a powerful, at times an almost unendurable, sense both of the complete believability of the violence and of its strangeness, its unnaturalness, its 'violation' aspect.[17]

In 'Looking Back on the Spanish Civil War', Orwell recalls an episode one dawn when he was out sniping:

At this moment a man, presumably carrying a message to an officer, jumped out of the trench and ran along the top of the parapet in full view. He was half-dressed and was holding up his trousers with both hands as he ran. I refrained from shooting at him. It is true that I am a poor shot and unlikely to hit a running man at a hundred yards, and also that I was thinking chiefly about getting back to our trench while the Fascists had their attention fixed on the aeroplanes. Still, I did not shoot because of that detail about the trousers. I had come here to shoot at 'Fascists'; but a man who is holding up his trousers isn't a 'Fascist', he is visibly a fellow creature, similar to yourself, and you don't feel like shooting at him.[18]

It is that sense of being confronted intimately with fellow creatures that makes so unbearable some of the prints in Jan Luiken's series on religious persecutions, especially the one in which a bearded priest, Leonard Keuser, reclining on the floor of the low cart taking him towards the stake in a field in the background, is pensively plucking a flower growing in the roadway.[19] And where the horrors of Nazi Europe are concerned, the same general principles apply. The reported horrors that especially lodge themselves in the memory are often those in which the enormity of the kind of violation of the natural or domestic order of things seizes one, as in Eichmann's reported recollection that 'A ditch had been there, which was already filled in. And there was, gushing from the earth, a spring of blood like a fountain . . .,' or the information that 'Deportation Rumanian style consisted in herding five thousand people into freight cars and letting them die there of suffocation while the train traveled through the countryside without plan or aim for days on end; a favorite follow-up to these killing operations was to expose the corpses in Jewish butcher shops.'[20] But much quieter details also have their effects. Bettelheim's information in *The Informed Heart* that at Dachau and Buchenwald in the late 1930s the prisoners' beds were covered with blue-and-white check coverlets which had to be kept flawlessly smooth and squared up during the day seems to me to do more to make those camps real than a good many far more dramatic details in other works.[21] And it is obvious why Wertham's eyes,

and no doubt those of a lot of other people, were held
by the central detail in the following passage:

> In Eglfing-Haar, which had an excellent reputation
> as a psychiatric hospital, there was a children's
> division with a capacity of about 150 children called
> the *Kinderhaus*. This division had a 'special
> department' with twenty-five beds and cribs for the
> children about to be exterminated. In June, 1945,
> it was still occupied by twenty children. They were
> saved by the American Army. In the children's
> 'special department' there was a small room. It was
> bare except for a small white-tiled table. At the
> window was a geranium plant which was always
> carefully watered. Four or five times a month a
> psychiatrist and a nurse took a child to this little
> room. A little while later they came out, alone.[22]

The special horror of trying to *increase* the normality of
settings in which horrors are perpetrated is brilliantly
conveyed in the section of Brownlow and Mollo's *It
Happened Here* dealing with the charming convalescent
home, with formal gardens and all, that is serving as a
euthanasia centre.

However, there is one further class of violations that I
shall touch on in this chapter, and they seem to me a
good deal more equivocal. I have in mind a number of
incidents in which one has a breaching of barriers which
may at first glance appear eminently natural ones, but
which on closer inspection involve the idea of status. For
example, I have heard more than one person comment,
rightly it seemed to me, that the most shocking moment
in Polanski's *Repulsion* was when Catherine Deneuve's
manicure clippers suddenly bit deliberately into the
finger of her beauty-parlour client. The deliberateness

was part of the shock, as was the extreme normality of the context in which the girl's madness was starting to manifest itself. But the most important reason, it seems to me, was the complete relaxation and trust in the presence of edged tools that had suddenly been violated, the sudden disruption of an entire social convention in which, by virtue of the mere fact of being a client, one was safe. (Hence too, of course, the peculiar fascination evoked for so many years in England by the figure of the throat-slitting Demon Barber, Sweeney Todd, and the special nastiness of the barbershop 'execution' in Windust's *The Enforcer* [*Murder Inc.* in England], and the flesh-creeping comic effectiveness of W. C. Fields in Sennett's *The Barber Shop*.) And up to a point one's sense of outrage is eminently justifiable. The closing shot of the Odessa Steps sequence in Eisenstein's *Battleship Potemkin*, for example, is especially shocking because the image of the sabred face of the respectably dressed middle-aged gentlewoman comes at the end of an absolute anthology of violences to the normally sacrosanct, including cripples and babies. And the dreadfulness of the cool gunning-down of Boggs by Colonel Sherburn in *Huckleberry Finn* resides in the way in which everything is working conventionally in the old man's favour so far as our sympathies are concerned – his harmlessness, his painful sobering up, his terror, the presence of his daughter hurrying forward to take him home. He too, one feels, pre-eminently doesn't deserve to become a victim at this point.

Nevertheless, the fact is that Boggs himself, in his gratuitous and repeated insulting of the Colonel earlier, has obviously been presuming a good deal too easily that the Colonel will not in reality do anything to him or carry out his pledge. And our instinctive recoil at the end of the Odessa Steps sequence entails, I think, an equally unsound presumption on our part that whatever may happen to the other people, this particular person shouldn't have been attacked: she wears glasses, she is serious-looking, she is one of us. And what certain violences do is to challenge illegitimate presumptions of inviolability. To give a not entirely frivolous example, it was refreshing when in Tenney's *The Horror of Party Beach* great black scaly Things came up out of the water and carried off screaming teenagers in contexts – rock-and-roll beach dancing, pajama parties, and so on – that normally served in such movies to reassure teenagers of their own admirableness and invulnerability by virtue of the mere fact of being between the ages of twelve and twenty. And something oddly similar occurs in the episode in *Wuthering Heights* in which, having lured Nelly Dean and young Cathy up to the Heights, Heathcliff casually pulls the latter to him, when she annoys him, and with his free hand 'administered . . . a shower of terrific slaps on both sides of the head' (ch. 27). The action is shocking, especially because of the implicit revelation that Cathy can from now on expect absolutely no mercy at the Heights by virtue of her various conventionally estimable statuses – daughter of respectable local citizen, pretty young girl, compassionate lover of an unhappy boy, heroine of this part of the novel, and so on. Indeed, the violence here is more disconcerting than some of the physically greater ones elsewhere in the book, just as the nose-pulling and ear-biting incidents in Dostoevsky's *The Possessed* carry a fuller charge of meaning than some of the far greater violences in his *Memoirs from the House of the Dead*, and just as the episode in which Tom Buchanan breaks Myrtle Wilson's nose in *The Great Gatsby* is more disturbing than the murder of Gatsby. Nevertheless, it is also plain that Cathy herself, like those other adolescents, has been presuming a little too much on the world's treating her benevolently. And there is no doubt, furthermore, that she has mentally dehumanized, or at least overconfidently categorized, the socially inferior Heathcliff, just as the injured middle-aged woman in the beauty parlour may have overconfidently categorized and dismissed from her thoughts the technician ministering to her vanity.[28] E. M. Forster, understood all this sort of thing unusually well; it is the chief point, for example, of the utterly 'indefensible' torturing of Philip by Gino in *Where Angels Fear to Tread*.

And this brings me to the more complicated problem of the figure of the violator.

VIOLATORS

What shocks one so deeply about a number of the violences that I have mentioned – the crucified lions in *Salammbô*, for instance, or the killing of Boggs, or the *Kinderhaus* at Eglfing-Haar – is not merely the sufferings and deaths of the innocent, or ignorant, or helpless. It is also the fact that other people have been able to commit those violences[1] and to ignore the traditional safeguards of innocence, and ignorance, and helplessness.[2] One has the sensation of a chasm having opened in front of one's feet. And the immediate reaction is to demand, How *could* they? How could they do it?

Such questions were given a special resonance by the post-1945 revelations of the Nazi horrors. They had no doubt been asked earlier of some of the more gratuitous murder cases, such as Leopold and Loeb's strangling of Bobby Franks in 1924, or the Papin sisters' butchering of their employers in 1933 (of which Genet made so timid a use in *Les bonnes*). But in the pre-war years, at least in Britain, the general attitude towards violence was untinged with metaphysical concerns. In 'The Decline of the English Murder', Orwell classically defines the appeal of a 'good murder' for readers of the *News of the World*; and the comparable demand by their social 'betters' for fictional murders seems to have been insatiable.[3] Implicit in this interest was a tacit acknowledgment that murder was usually quite understandable and, in a sense, quite natural. Husbands killed wives because they wanted their money, or were tired of being nagged, or wished to go off with someone else. Wives killed husbands out of jealousy, or to get their freedom, an attitude that François Mauriac found perfectly comprehensible in *Thérèse Desqueyroux*. Relatives, business associates, social acquaintances, and so on, killed each other for gain, or from fear of blackmail, and the like. And on a more public plane, the reasons for extreme violence were equally uncomplicated. Either groups or nations wanted things belonging to other ones and tried to take them; or they behaved in the spirit of the Duke in James Thurber's *The Thirteen Clocks*, who remarked that 'We all have our flaws, and mine is being wicked.' Romans martyred Christians because they were decadent, Spanish Inquisitors burned heretics because they were religious bigots, American Indians tortured prisoners because they were savages, German troops committed atrocities in Belgium in 1914 because they were Huns,[4] brownshirts beat up Jews because they were antisemitic and so on. Violences, thus considered, were not a problem intellectually: the overwhelming majority of people in civilized countries didn't commit them, civilized states didn't commit them, and their perpetrators obviously couldn't offer defences of them that would carry even a tincture of validity for civilized people.

The large-scale revelations from Nazi Europe caused the collapse of those certainties for the even moderately reflective. On the one hand there was the politicization of violence, the incorporation of atrocious violences into the very fabric of society, and hence a demonstration of the possibility of the legitimation of the illegal, the centralization of the eccentric. And on the other, given the large number of perfectly ordinary people involved in one way or another in the perpetration of hitherto unthinkable horrors, there was the disquieting intimation, not only that there are latent possibilities for frightfulness in a great many people, but that relatively small shifts in social structures can permit those possibilities to realize themselves. Hence, faced since then with particularly shocking instances of violence – the 'Moors' case, say, or the *Clockwork Orange* kind of vandalism, or the activities of American troops in My Lai – it has been impossible not to feel concerned about where such things might lead us. And that concern naturally affects one's thinking about some of the violences in art.

Nevertheless, there is an important paradox that must be kept in mind here. Art can indeed help to alert one to alarming possibilities, both in groups and individuals. And presentations of violence can help us to understand more fully the natures of various kinds of violators, and of attitudes that make for violation, and so, in the long run, help us to be better able to deal with them. But an essential condition is that one empathizes with the perpetrators of the violences, however much one may deplore or abominate the violences themselves. I am not speaking of the kind of understanding provided by studies like Lewis Yablonsky's *The Violent Gang*,[5] valuable as they may be, nor even of the kind that a writer like Laing provides. In the rest of this chapter I shall try to explain what I mean.

In Flaubert's 'La Légende de Saint Julien l'Hospitalier', there is an oddly disquieting little paragraph. It occurs in the section describing how Julien, the young nobleman, becomes an obsessed, insatiable, and pitiless hunter riding out alone each day, and is simply this: 'Bientôt, il entra dans un bois. Au bout d'une branche, un coq de bruyère engourdi par le froid dormait la tête sous l'aile. Julien, d'un revers d'épée, lui faucha les deux pattes, et sans le ramasser continua sa route.' ('Soon he entered a wood. At the end of a branch a grouse, benumbed by the cold, was sleeping with its head under its wing. With a backhand stroke of his sword, Julien sliced off its feet and, without picking it up, continued on his way.') On the face of it, the reasons why the passage is disquieting are plain. One not only feels in imagination the defencelessness of the creature huddled up against the cold, the shock of its awakening, the hopelessness of its frantic struggles on the ground, the certainty of its death by starvation or in the grip of a predator. One also feels the casual deliberateness of the sword stroke, the indifference of the horseman as he rides away from the floundering bird, and the utter impossibility of getting through to him should a comparable whim have taken him about a larger creature – oneself. But something else also happens. The fact is that one *does* enter into the impulse of the sword stroke, and into Julien's frame of mind as he continues his quest for other victims. And the same kind of thing occurs with a number of the other violences that I have been talking about so far, such as Heathcliff's, or Gino's, or even Sherburn's. In other words, one is in some degree simultaneously the victim of the violences, one's own consciously-judging, civilized self being shocked by them, *and* the violator.

Now, to talk about this topic, and about the question of empathy, provides more opportunities for unintended ironies than almost any other. And any sedentary intellectual venturing upon it should have firmly at the back of his mind Heathcliff's sardonic comment upon the attitude of the romantic sentimentalist Isabella towards himself before their marriage: 'But no brutality disgusted her – I suppose, she has an innate admiration of it, if only her precious person were secure from injury!' (ch. 14). Where art is concerned, this kind of sentimentality is to be seen the most clearly at times in the French cult of the Sadean, as in a passage like the following, by Robert Benayoun in the journal *Présence du cinéma:*

> Il est indispensable d'ajouter que le vrai sadique
> considère la constrainte, non comme un instrument
> d'injustice, ou d'oppression, mais comme une
> épreuve de caractéres. . . . Il lui est impossible par
> example, sauf par une erreure fatale, de soumettre
> des esprits libres comme le sien: il en deviendrait à
> son tour la victime. . . . Nous sommes ici à l'opposé
> du bourreau insensible, ou du dégéneré criminel:
> notre héros est généralement d'une culture
> approfondie, d'une courtoisie insolente, il manifeste
> le plus souvent un humour de belle qualité,
> conçoit le crime comme une oeuvre d'art et d'amour
> ('Tout ce que signe Sade est amour', dit Gilbert
> Lely), et accepte loyalement les règles de son
> propre jeu, jusqu'à en devenir la
> victime.[6]

Much the same attitude manifests itself in *Histoire d'O* and Georges de Coulteray's *Le sadisme au cinéma*; and, faced with it, one can only say, 'Show me.'

To be sure, there have been people in Renaissance Italy, for example, or Imperial China, or India, who combined great cruelty with a highly developed aesthetic sense. But the only actual historical person who, so far as I know, has been adduced as a Sadean 'hero' is Gilles de Rais, with perhaps the Hungarian countess Erzsébet Báthory as a runner up;[7] and it seems obvious that, far from playing composedly in any kind of game, both of them were as uncontrollably compulsive in their torture-killings as a plebeian sadist like Neville Heath or a number of the frenzied figures described by Sade himself. Furthermore, the two instances that I have come across that seem to approximate most nearly to the general mood of *Juliette* are ones that would be unlikely to win Surrealist approval. One is the case of the Mexican sisters who for over ten years, up to the raiding of their *hacienda* by the police in 1964, operated a private prison camp in which recalcitrant girls were broken in by torture and starvation for brothels, and who appear to have done to death well over thirty girls in the course of their operations. The other is that of the Juliette-like White Russian princess, the mistress of one of the heads of the French Gestapo during the Occupation, who among other things gave lavish parties for collaborationists and German officials that culminated in drunken visits to the cells downstairs in her house to make fun of prisoners who had been recently tortured or to see them tortured anew. (Like Juliette, she appears to have made a great deal of money through her activities.)[8] Furthermore, a good many of the fictional figures with an intense, ruthless, and relatively controlled urge to torment and destroy seem to me strikingly unsusceptible of sentimentalization. I am thinking of ones like the gunmen in *High Noon*, the hoodlums played by Lee Marvin in Lang's *The Big Heat* and Sturges' *Bad Day at Black Rock*, Robert Ryan's antisemite in Dmytryk's *Crossfire*, a number of the sociopaths in the novels of MacDonald and McPartland, Anthony Quayle's treasure-hunter in Guillermin's *Tarzan's Great Adventure*, Robert Russell's torturer in Reeves' *Witchfinder General*, Glenn Ford's hanging judge in Levin's *The Man from Colorado*, and the bandits in Barreto's *O Cangaceiro*. And it is obvious that they are far closer than Count Zaroff or Réage's preposterous bare-genitalled clubmen to such figures as the terrifying Ezzelino da Romano, thirteenth-century ruler of Padua, or the fourteenth-century ruler of Milan, Bernabó Visconti, and no doubt a good many other aristocratic figures with an undeflectable bent towards hurting and destroying.[9]

Furthermore, Sade himself was in part a sentimentalist. As Simone de Beauvoir puts it in 'Must We Burn Sade?': 'There was one dream common to most young aristocrats of the time. Scions of a declining class which had once possessed concrete power, but which no longer retained any real hold on the world, they tried to revive symbolically, in the privacy of the bedchamber, the status for which they were nostalgic: that of the lone and sovereign feudal despot.'[10] But it is also patent how firmly Sade is based in his own century. The power that permits *his* murderers and torturers to enjoy themselves endlessly in their castles or abbeys is not the military prowess of themselves and their peers but, quite simply, money. And, to judge from the striking ineptness with which he conducted his own life, it seems clear that he himself could not have survived in a warrior culture. The attacks made in *Juliette* on the central ideal of such a culture, namely physical courage, seem done with conviction, as do the related attacks on duelling. And if one of the two model societies that Sade imagined in *Aline et Valcour*, and that obviously corresponded to one of the two principal aspects of his thinking was, as Pierre Favre puts it in *Sade utopiste*, 'a loosely-knit feudal system like that which existed in France before the year 1000' (p. 16),[11] the male characters in his works, with the possible exception of the ogre Minsky in *Juliette*, are vastly different from the warrior type to be found in that period. As Guy Molino shrewdly notes, Sade's real heroes are women.[12]

Nevertheless, Sade's work does direct one's attention to important facts, both in what he accomplishes and in what he fails to accomplish. And what particularly interests me at this point is his own sense, as manifested in the progression inside his work from *Les cent vingt jours* to *Juliette* and in the progression inside *Juliette*, that mere compulsive violence and violation, even if the compulsions need to be acknowledged and allowed for in social thinking, are ultimately of little interest, and that what ultimately *is of interest* is the kind of violence that is perpetrated by coherent personalities acting autonomously and intelligently. And while in Sade's own work the attempt to separate the two kinds of violence and make the controlled kind part of a lucid and invulnerable philosophical system is clearly a failure, his emphasis still seems to me correct. Let me draw on horror movies again to make clearer what I mean.

Essentially there are two sharply different kinds of movie 'monsters'. On the one hand, there are beings who have crossed the border between the 'human' and the 'monstrous', or are in the process of doing so, and who are the victims of forces outside their control. The most obvious examples are werewolves, vampires, zombies, Jekyll–Hyde, Frankenstein's various creations, and such occasional non-generic figures as the spore-infested returned astronaut of Guest's *The Quatermass Experiment*; and the long artistic lives of most of them testify to their having embodied anxieties which most of us have felt from time to time about our own psychic stability. The correspondences, however, are crude, and the figures have mostly proven very vulnerable to parody. And when a use is made of more natural monsters of this kind, as in *Psycho*, Aldrich's *Whatever Happened to Baby Jane?*, and a number of similar works, the result is either Grand Guignol or, as in *Repulsion*, the kind of clinical rendering of insanity that, whatever anxieties one may have had about one's own mind, helps to bring home how the peculiar awfulness of certain kinds of madness is precisely that the affected persons have crossed a frontier beyond which, unless one happens to be an uncommonly gifted psychiatrist like Laing, one cannot follow them. Yeats' disdain for passive suffering seems to me to carry over logically to certain kinds of infliction of suffering – the kinds, I mean, that issue out of states of confusion, disarray, an overall lowering of psychological effectiveness, as in a passage like the following from *Memoirs from the House of the Dead*:

> So I grabs her by the hair; her plaits were so thick and long and I twisted them round my hand and I squeezed her between my knees from behind and I took out my knife and bent her head back and I cut her throat like a calf. . . . She screamed and the blood just spouted out and I threw my knife down and put my arms round her and I laid down on the ground with my arms round her and I yelled and roared over her; she was screaming and I was screaming; she was all wriggling and struggling out of my arms, and the blood was all on me, the blood – it was just pouring all over my face and over my hands as well, just pouring . . . (pp. 216–17).[13]

One is drawn initially into a sort of shocked empathy, but the states of consciousness involved are almost inevitably less well articulated and less clear than one's own consciousness normally is; and so, denied any real clarification and advance in understanding, one sooner or later simply withdraws from involvement. Far from being too exciting, explosive, and challenging, genuine derangement, whether in actuality or in art, is mostly too inward-turning, and hence simply not interesting enough. And the violences of deranged persons seem to me still essentially inward-looking, in that the victims do not really figure in them in terms of their own identities, but in terms of whatever particular delusional system the violator is working in terms of.

There is, however, a second kind of central figure in a number of horror movies, and this seems to me the more important of the two, namely the totally committed and self-controlled figure gripped by an obsession in the pursuit of which he will shrink from absolutely no violences or atrocities that seem necessary. Dr Genessier of *Les yeux sans visage*, Baron Frankenstein as played by Peter Cushing, the plastic surgeon, Dr Schuler, of Hayer's *Circus of Horrors*, the black magician of Tourneur's *Night of the Demon*, and of course Count Zaroff – these and others like them are the truly disquieting figures. Their conduct is iniquitous, certainly. But the atrocities that they commit or are responsible for issue from co-herent, unified personalities functioning with complete certainty and, in a sense, *non*-monstrously. That is to say, they are not patently crippled, deformed, contemptible, or pitiable like the figures in the first group, and up to a point they are capable of functioning perfectly success-fully in normal society.

And what applies in horror movies applies even more strongly elsewhere. The more ordered and channelled the energies making for violence are, the more significant the violences themselves are likely to be, and the more enlightening the entailed empathy. The following pass-age, for example, quoted by Robert M. Coates in *Outlaw Years* and recounting the end of Big Harpe at the hands of a man whose wife and child the Harpes had mur-dered a day or two earlier, grips the mind a good deal more than the one from *The House of the Dead*:

Stegall took Harp's own butcher knife, which Leiper had compelled him to deliver up, and taking Harp by the hair of the head, drew the knife slowly across

the back of his neck, cutting to the bone; Harp
staring him full in the face, with a grim and fiendish
countenance, and exclaiming, 'You are a God
Damned rough butcher, but cut on and be damned!'

Stegall then passed the knife around his neck,
cutting to the bone; and then wrung off his head, in
the same manner a butcher would of a hog ... (p. 66).

And a similar implacability is discernible, at a much
higher level, in Bosch's *The Crowning with Thorns* in
the London National Gallery. The two tormentors of
Christ in the lower half of the painting are merely
repulsive: they put one in mind of some of Sade's gar-
rulous and cowardly voluptuaries, hidden away inside
the black-fairy-tale security of walls and money from the
threats of other males and even from the kind of social
risks run by Valmont in Choderlos de Laclos' *Les liaisons
dangereuses*. But the other two tormentors in the pic-
ture – the clean-shaven, neatly accoutred, grave-looking
military figures – are not only genuinely frightening;
they are frightening in part because they are eminently
respectable and in some degree *deserve* respect. And
obviously one could have found their equivalents in the
Waffen S.S. or Massu's paratroopers or in other organized
bodies of professionally violent men whose activities one
particularly abominates or dreads.

Having said that – having pointed to one of the most
extreme instances that one can imagine – I would like to
look more directly at the question of Nazism.

Confronted with the Nazi atrocities – confronted, even
more, with the kinds of utterly unrepentant and unrecon-
structable former torturers on display in Peter Weiss's
'oratorio' *The Interrogation* – it is natural enough to feel
with the narrator of Jorge Semprun's *The Long Voyage*
that 'there's no point trying to understand the S.S.; it

suffices to exterminate them'.[14] But I think that this attitude, nowadays at least, is a mistake. As Helmut Krausnick puts it in *Anatomy of the SS State*:

Since Hitler's dictatorship is so obviously to be condemned from all points of view, people are tempted to think too little about it. This is why, although we possess an immense mass of literature about the Third Reich, so little intelligent use has been made of it. The superficiality of many works on the subject is no more than a reflection of the popular tendency; people prefer vivid writing (and it is difficult not to write vividly about Auschwitz); people try to evade the rationalism of the historian and prefer moralistic emotional theorizing. The current phrase [in 1965] is 'conscience awakening'. But a sleepy conscience is like a sleepy man: if a man is shaken hard enough he will wake up – and then after one or two half-waking moments will quickly go to sleep again. That which man's intellect once grasps however will remain and will not disappear.[15]

And one can see why it is that the conscience that is aroused without being led to understanding does go back to sleep. As I suggested earlier, one of the more dismaying aspects of the Nazi horrors is the way in which their impact has diminished as the years have gone by. An important factor in this, it seems to me, has almost certainly been the paucity until recently of distinguished works of art that presented Nazis and the Nazi *Weltanschauung* with the kind of empathy necessary for bringing things out of the realm of nightmarish quasi-natural disasters and into a daylight where one's full intelligence could come to bear on them – come to bear as it can on figures like Macbeth, and Edmund in *King Lear*. Looking back on the inception of his and Andrew Mollo's brilliant filmic imagining, *It Happened Here*, of what England might have been like three or four years after a British surrender to Hitler in 1940, Kevin Brownlow recalled that:

> The Nazi era was as forbidden a subject at that time [the mid 1950s] as pornography to the Victorians. Neither of us had yet developed an understanding of National Socialism; we shared the general horror at their crimes, but were fascinated by the unexplained elements of the Nazi phenomenon. I have never been able to analyse this. Both of us are inordinately squeamish. We cringe at the sight of a hospital uniform. Nazism should have repelled us with its constant reminders of brutality. But mysteries continued to cloud the era. And mystery is a powerful attraction.[16]

That such an attitude has been fairly common seems testified to by the recent spate of works dealing with the subject – paperback novels, pictorial histories, straight histories, movies, and so on. Moreover, there is a significant difference between some of the present works and earlier ones on the subject.

'Everything's coming up Adolf Hitler these days,' A. H. Weiler commented in the *New York Times* in 1972, contemplating De Concini's *Hitler: the Last Ten Days* (with Alec Guinness), and other projected works. And one of the clearest signals about the shift of attitude entailed, particularly in New York, was the apparent acceptability three or four years ago of Brooks' *The Producers*, in which a couple of shyster New York entrepreneurs attempt to lose money by putting on the most offensive production that they can devise, namely a musical entitled 'Springtime for Hitler', only to find it become a sell-out success as a comedy, S.S. uniforms, rally banners, and all. The movie was in sickeningly bad taste, but that is beside the point. The point is that for a good many people the unthinkable has as suddenly been becoming thinkable. There are no doubt several reasons for this, among them the use of Storm-Trooper-like tactics by 'good' groups like the S.D.S. and some of the Black militants, the reversal in the Middle East since 1967 in which, after its *Blitzkrieg* victory, Israel has found itself in a role ironically similar in some ways to that of the Nazis in occupied Europe, and the analogies between American conduct in Vietnam and that of the Nazis, with the related sharpening of interest in the general question of the decent citizen's complicity in the crimes of his country. But in any case, it is obviously becoming easier for people to acknowledge certain ambivalences in their attitude towards Nazism.

As I indicated earlier, however, there are dangers in this kind of swing. And it is important to understand what is being empathized with, and to what extent that empathy is legitimate. This necessitates appreciating the kinds of energies involved. Movies like Bertolucci's *The Conformist* and Petri's *Investigation of a Citizen above Suspicion*, with their emphasis on the emptiness, the instability, the joylessness of Fascist types, seem to me to permit the viewer too easy a sense of moral superiority. No doubt various kinds of instability were often involved. They appear, for instance, to have characterized such intellectual French collaborationists as Robert Brasillach and Pierre Drieu la Rochelle (who in Sartre's words 'wanted Fascism for society, when all he needed to do was to apply strict rules of behaviour to himself'[17]), and to be observable on the screen in the figure of the aristocrat

Mazières in Ophuls' *Le chagrin et la pitié* (*The Sorrow and the Pity*). But obviously a good deal more was involved, and to enquire what it was does not entail moving far, if at all, from the subject of art. Nazism itself was more conscious of the visual – of icons and designs, of costuming and pageantry, of 'theatre' – than any other political movement has been. And we have not only had the presentation of this aspect of it in a plethora of photographs and newsreels, as well as in Riefenstahl's *Olympiad 1936* and *Triumph of the Will*. We have also had such an abundance of fictional treatments of the subject that the black-uniformed blonde S.S. man and the trench-coated Gestapo man have become part of almost everyone's consciousness.

As I have said, our sense of fearsome possibilities in both societies and individuals was greatly extended by Nazism, and it was extended in at least three directions. One was the sheer delight that some people take in inflicting frightful cruelties on others in the sort of relationship that Sartre discusses at one point in *What is Literature?* and that Baudelaire epitomizes in the line 'Le bourreau qui jouit, le martyr qui sanglote' ('the torturer enjoying himself, the martyr sobbing'). It is what one sees, for example, in Kogon's account of the S.S. Master Sergeant in the Buchenwald prison block who 'admitted some 150 murders within a single half year'; who 'would, for example, force the stripped prisoner to immerse his testicles in ice-cold and boiling water in turn, painting them with iodine when the skin came off in strips'; and who 'at night . . . would sometimes summon a victim from one of the cells and leisurely do away with him in [his] room. He would then place the body under his bed and fall asleep peacefully, his work well done.'[18]

The second direction is the demonstration, most obvious in the elite troops of the Waffen S.S., of the continuing appeal of the warrior spirit and ethos described by Nietzsche in *The Genealogy of Morals*, especially in the following passage:

> These same men who, amongst themselves, are so strictly constrained by custom, worship, ritual, gratitude, and by mutual surveillance and jealousy, who are so resourceful in consideration, tenderness, loyalty, pride and friendship, when once they step outside their circle become little better than uncaged beasts of prey. Once abroad in the wilderness, they revel in the freedom from social constraint and compensate for their long confinement in the quietude of their own community. They revert to the innocence of wild animals: we can imagine them returning from an orgy of murder, arson, rape, and torture, jubilant and at peace with themselves as though they had committed a fraternity prank – convinced, moreover, that the poets for a long time to come will have something to sing about and to praise.[19]

And the third is the bureaucratic dreadfulness, the thing that Arendt defined so brilliantly in her discussion of Eichmann, and that appears to have caught at one point the eye of Godard, who, according to Richard Roud,

> once wanted to make a film about the concentration camps, but one which would be seen from the side of the torturers, as it were. It would be concerned with the practical, everyday problems: how to incinerate twenty bodies for the price of ten – cutting down on gas, etc. We would see typists carefully making their inventories of hair, teeth, etc.

What would have been unbearable about such scenes, said Godard, was not the horror of them, but on the contrary, their completely normal and everyday aspect.[20]

Of the three kinds of ruthlessness the third is obviously by far the most dangerous now. It is what has manifested itself not only in the bureaucracy of the Final Solution, but in recent American military policy, in a lot of corporate business activity, in the running of institutions of confinement where no pressure is put on those in control to behave decently, and in the thinking of too many urban planners, behavioural psychologists, and other would-be rationalizers and manipulators. And entailed in it is almost always an attempted denial of, or averting of eyes from, the actual intensity of suffering, the experience of the suffering consciousness, usually in the name of some higher good. Whereas the other two, in their pure forms, involve a heightened sense of the consciousness of other people – for the first, as victims, for the second, as antagonists – the third involves a willed and in some measure theoretically supported denial or ignoring of individual identities, complexities, and differentiating modes of feelings. Hence, no doubt, the spotlessness of so many Nazi consciences. The bureaucratic exterminators were in effect willing their victims to be their individual selves as little as possible and to *feel* as little as possible; and hence any sufferings that occurred could be considered the result of a kind of perverse wilfulness on the part of the sufferers.

Moreover, the bureaucratic aspect is doubly dangerous because of its relationship to the technocratic. It is a great pity that Godard never made his projected movie. It might have been his masterpiece, and one of the most disquieting aspects of it could have been the involvement, the unwilling sympathetic involvement, of the audience in the problem-solving, skill-displaying aspects of those activities. One of the unfortunate things about the most common cliché image of the camps – the shaven-headed prisoner being whipped to work by the glossy-booted S.S. man – is its falsity to the wartime actuality of the great camps, with their complex bureaucracies operated to a very large extent by the prisoners themselves, with all the struggles for power, prestige, and privilege which one finds inside any bureaucracy.[21] The camps were brilliant, terrible organizations. They were not *sui generis*, they were the ultimate extreme of features of other organizations – military, para-military, business, educational even. And part of their sinister fascination is what is also exerted by the complexities of the S.S. as an organization, or the complexities of the organization of the Nazi party, particularly in its relation to the traditional bureaucratic structure, to the armed forces, and to German industry. It is the twin fascination of organizational ingenuity and complexity, and of the pleasurableness and drama of exercising power and jockeying for greater power inside such a system or set of overlapping systems.[22] And of course there was all the technological ingenuity too.[23] It is a heady mixture. As movies like Visconti's *The Damned* have begun to intimate, Nazism and Fascism are capable of providing present-day artists with some of the opportunities that the politics of Imperial Rome provided for those of Tudor and Jacobean England.

However, it is the other two aspects of Nazism – the psychopathological and the martial – that concern me more here, especially in their relation to Sadeanism. The resemblances between certain aspects of Sadeanism and Nazism have often been remarked upon, and it is desirable to be clearly aware of them. Geoffrey Gorer seems right when he observes in *The Life and Ideas of the Marquis de Sade* that in the Europe of *Juliette*, Sade 'exposes a system of corruption and intrigue together with a hard-heartedness and sanctimonious cynicism which might have served as a model to Hitler's Germany'.[24] Camus seems right when he observes in *The Rebel* that 'the reduction of man to an object of experiment, the rule which specifies the relation between the will to power and man as an object, the sealed laboratory which is the scene of this monstrous experiment, are lessons which the theoreticians of power will learn again [after Sade's time] when they have to organize the age of slavery'.[25] Raymond Queneau seems right when he observed in 1945 that 'It is incontestable that the world imagined by Sade and desired by his characters (and why not by himself?) is a hallucinatory foreshadowing of the world ruled over by the Gestapo, with its tortures and its camps.'[26]

At the same time, however, the indignation provoked in French admirers of Sade by such identifications cannot simply be written off as an instance of the oddness of French intellectuals. If the author of the most illuminating and best-reputed discussion of Sade, Maurice Blanchot, was a member in the 1930s of one of the nonconformist Rightist groups,[27] Sade's most enthusiastic and consistent supporters have always been the Surrealists, whose anti-Fascist record has been exemplary. And the Surrealists' support cannot simply be attributed to the protean quality of Sade's thinking, from which it is possible to extract two radically opposed positions.[28] Or, if it can, it isn't in a straightforward way. André Breton, as usual, seems to have provided the essential clue in his observation in *Anthologie de l'humour noir* that: 'One of the greatest poetic virtues of [Sade's] work is to set the depiction of social iniquities and human perversions in

the light of the phantasmagorias and terrors of childhood,
at the risk of sometimes leading them to become con-
fused with each other.'[29] It is true that the nearest thing
in political terms to the relationship between the individual and his environment that Sade delineates so often –
the ruthless egoism, the insistence on the right to the
gratification of one's every desire, the insatiable will
towards dominance, the insistence on the inferiority of all
one's victims, the continual breaking of alliances, the
wholly opportunistic use of whatever tactics or pleas will
best serve at each moment, and the conviction that all
this is inevitably part of the natural order of things – is
the relationship between Nazi Germany and the rest of
Europe that Hitler defined in *Mein Kampf* and subsequently tried to put into practice. But it is also plain
that Hitler's thinking frequently corresponded to what
Ernst Nolte in his *Three Faces of Fascism* calls 'the child
who is aware of nothing except himself and his mental
image and to whom time means nothing because
childishness has not been broken and forced into the
sober give-and-take of the adult world'.[30] And if the
Thousand-Year Reich makes one think of Gorer's observation that Sade 'had created a world, or a hell, where all
wishes could be realized, where every fantasy of love and
hate could be made real, where one received only such
punishment as one desired, and where the will, the
intellect, the passions, and the lusts held undisputed
sway' (pp. 212–13), it seems plain that the resemblances
are not due to any intellectual influence of one man on
another, but to the fact that in Sade and Hitler alike one
has extreme examples of childlike sociopathic thinking, the
one in sexual-intellectual terms, the other in political ones.

However, one cannot stop at that point: the appeal –
and to some extent the valid appeal – of that kind of
thinking has also to be allowed for. Illimitable energies,

perfect good health, an undamageable body, continuous good luck, unshakeable self-confidence, completely re-alizable ambitions, victims who never, ever, rebel, barriers that invariably yield, choices that are never hard to make, inexhaustible sexual vitality, unflagging sexual gratification – which of us, carried up to a high place and offered those things with nothing to pay and no strings attached, would immediately and unhesitatingly turn them down, unless aspiring to a greater fulness of being in some other world? It is this image of the good life that Sade proffers, above all in *Juliette*, if one is only man or woman enough to go after it with total commitment and absolute philosophical clarity. And of course it is a corresponding vision in political terms that Hitler offers. 'I free mankind', he reportedly claimed at one point, 'from the yoke of reason which weighs upon it, from the obscene and humiliating intoxications derived from chimeras, from so-called conscience and morality . . .';[31] and it is obviously very agreeable to think of oneself as being a totally different kind of person from what one is, free of inhibiting introspection, self-distrust, confused and conflicting yearnings and timidities ('awkward, pasty, feeling the draught/ [With] health and strength and beauty on the brain,' as W. H. Auden put it in *Look Stranger*). One can understand how Auden, looking back in 1966 on one of his works from the early 1930s, could have been moved to comment that his name on the title page 'seems a pseudonym for someone else, someone talented but near the border of sanity, who might well, in a year or two, become a Nazi'.[32]

But one can also see that more than merely quasi-infantile yearnings were involved in what Pol Van-dromme, speaking of Drieu la Rochelle, calls 'that sombre poetry which fascism had been for some of the men of his generation'.[33] If the roster of authors who at some point were sympathetic towards Fascism is substantial – for example, Heidegger, Céline, Pound, Hamsun, D'Annunzio, Yeats, Maurras, Marinetti, Gentile, Pirandello, Drieu la Rochelle, Marcel Jouhandeau, Wyndham Lewis, Cocteau, Jünger, Gottfried Benn – [34] this is partly because Fascism, 'that thoroughly ambiguous ideology' as Alastair Hamilton calls it in *The Appeal of Fascism*, offered to satisfy genuine and respectable human needs. 'The deepest definition of Fascism is this,' Drieu la Rochelle observes; 'it is the political movement which leads most frankly, most radically towards the restoration of the body – health, dignity, fulness, heroism – towards the defence of man against the large town and the machine.'[35] And the more insidious appeal lurking in Nazism is the way in which it can stir up an unacknowledged measure of sympathy with energy, power, freedom from certain inhibitions, and (for a substantial period anyway, which is what matters when one is talking about consciousness) success and the unperturbed enjoyment of martial or quasi-martial power. Visconti's *The Damned* brilliantly catches an aspect of this, particularly in his handling of the S.S. man Von Aschenbach; so does *It Happened Here*, with its bringing home of the very tangible everyday advantages of belonging to the party; so at a much lower level, does 'Sarban's' fantasy novel, *The Sound of His Horn*, set in a Europe that has had a hundred years of the New Order; and so, of course, where the Nazis' own art is concerned, does Riefenstahl's magisterial filming of the 1934 Nuremberg rally, with its culminating exhilarated singing of the Horst Wessel song in a way calculated to leave that tune permanently impressed on one's memory.

Nor can the appeal of the martial and heroic be lightly dismissed. It is easy enough to object that it was precisely the Nietzschean celebration of violence which, vul-

garized, helped to encourage the kind of outlook in the
S.S. that resulted in conduct to which the passage that I
quoted earlier from Nietzsche was all too applicable. It
is easy enough, too, to diagnose the adolescent attitudes
displayed in the 1914–18 journals of the genuinely heroic
proto-Nazi Ernst Jünger,[36] in contrast to what one finds in
R. H. Tawney's 'Some Reflections of a Soldier',[37] or
Robert Graves' *Goodbye to All That*. It is also easy
enough to identify the kind of emotional instability that
attracted figures like Drieu la Rochelle and Brasillach
into collaboration with the Nazis. But it is still no less the
case that Nietzsche's account, in its essentials, has held
true of a good many warriors and warrior-communities
and that the problematic intermingling of values in warfare has been attested to by men a good deal more
distinguished as thinkers than Jünger.

If it was Jünger ('the only man of superior culture who
gave Nazism even the appearance of being a philosophy',
according to Camus in *The Rebel*, p. 149) who observed
that 'time only strengthens my conviction that it was a
good and strenuous life, and that the war, for all its
destructiveness, was an incomparable schooling of the
heart',[38] it was one of the founders of socialism, Pierre-
Joseph Proudhon, who observed that 'war is the basis of
our history, our life, and our whole being. It is, I repeat,
everything.'[39] And it was that eminently civilized phil-
osopher William James who in 'The Moral Equivalent of
War' pointed out in 1910 that 'showing war's irrationality
and horror is of no effect upon [modern man]. The
horrors make the fascination. War is the *strong* life; it is
life *in extremis*', and who suggested that 'pacifists ought
to enter more deeply into the aesthetical and ethical
point of view of their opponents'.[40]

From the point of view of undercutting jingoism or militarism we obviously cannot have too many treatments

of warfare like Franju's *Hôtel des Invalides,* or Watkins' *The War Game,* or, to judge from Ado Kyrou's account of it in *Le surréalisme au cinéma,* Huston's *Let There Be Light.* At the same time, however, art serves to remind us both of the conviction and enjoyment with which some men fight, and of the larger complexities of the subject. Where the First World War is concerned two anonymous photographs from 1914 do as much as volumes of contemporary patriotic rhetoric to bring home to one how solid was the structure of martial feelings created by two or three decades of militarism. One is a superb shot of soldiers in a French regiment swinging along jauntily under full packs through a city street and bantering with a couple of happy, admiring girls who have darted out to them from the watching crowd. The other is an uncannily similar one of German troops leaving likewise for the front – cheerful, good natured, similarly informed with that enviable kind of untroubled, casual masculine energy and certainty that appears to have been so marked a pre-1914 phenomenon.[41] Regardless of whether they were in error about what they expected to find, it is inescapable that in both pictures one is observing *warriors* going off to something exciting, something wished for, something eminently proper.[42]

Furthermore, while it is natural, especially in these days of the barely receding Vietnam horror, to think of war as mere butchery and brutalization, to do so is untrue to too many actualities. There are moral dimensions to warfare that it is dangerous to lose sight of, among them the way in which the discarding of various moral worries can sometimes (as in *The Red Badge of Courage*) result not only in greater efficiency as a fighting man but in a moral improvement as well; or the fact that rigid discipline can sometimes in the long run preserve morale, save lives, and even (if David Douglas Duncan's moving book of photographs from Korea, *This is War*, is to be trusted) not necessarily brutalize those who have been exposed to it; or the by no means ignoble exhilaration that battle can arouse (as in *War and Peace*, Frederic Manning's *The Middle Parts of Fortune*, and Guy Chapman's *A Passionate Prodigality*); or the enlargement of consciousness that it can bring (as in Isaac Rosenberg's poetry and Isaac Babel's *Red Cavalry*); or, in Hannah Arendt's words in *On Violence*, 'the well-known phenomenon of brotherhood on the battlefield, where the noblest, most selfless deeds are often daily occurrences' (p. 67); or the visual drama and beauty of warfare, as analysed, along with so much else, in J. Glenn Gray's magnificent phenomenological study of war, *The Warriors*.[43]

Without an inward understanding of such phenomena, it is difficult to cope with the appeal of the 'heroic'. And unless this is faced honestly, there is all too likely to be sentimentality, or callousness, or both when morally complex situations arise. As Orwell reminded us in discussing the recrudescence during the Spanish Civil War of those very attitudes that the 'right–left' people had been sneering at apropos of the 1914 war, the mind is prone to take advantage of opportunities for feeling things that it is enjoyable to feel. And part of the high intelligence of *Hôtel des Invalides* was that in the magnificent travelling shot through the great hall of armour, to the accompaniment of stirring martial music, Franju acknowledged to the full the Napoleonic appeal of *la gloire* – and then undercut our gratefully relaxing acquiescence in the feeling by confronting us with the mutilated war heroes in the chapel. Nor is the notion of a moral dimension at the centre of the heroic necessarily a delusion. Hector, Beowulf, Gunnar of the Njal Saga, the Knight of Chaucer's *Prologue*, Gawain of *Sir*

Gawain and the Green Knight, the Lancelot of the latter part of Malory, Sir Philip Sidney, Robert E. Lee, the great chiefs of the Plains Indians, and so on – the figure of the admirable warrior who stands at one corner of a triangle, equally distant from the dehumanizing bureaucrat and the deranged and compulsive sexual sadist, has always stirred men's hearts and imaginations, and will no doubt continue to do so: the continuing popularity of the Western among people of all political persuasions is testimony enough to that.

However, a further problem lurks here. Art also gives us reminders that men of violence whose actions one particularly abominates may in fact be personally likeable, or at least charming. Helmut Griem's Von Aschenbach in Visconti's *The Damned* carries conviction, for example, as does the Nazi officer that Griem portrays in Johnson's *The McKenzie Break*, and as do a variety of villains in thrillers, Westerns, and gangster movies. And it was obviously not accidental but central that in *Lear* Shakespeare should have made so likeable the supreme spokesman in his *oeuvre* for the philosophical system that supports and justifies not only Edmund's own machinations and violences and those of such other articulate and witty men of violence as Iago and Richard III, but the violences of Goneril and Regan. It is also not accidental that the term 'hero' is employed for figures like Ahab and Heathcliff. They too are not in any obvious sense deformed or monstrous, their value-systems and aspirations are coherent and intelligible, and one can continue empathizing with them even when they go the limit in terms of those systems. It is in fact precisely through this kind of embodying and vitalizing of value-systems that the fullest challenges and most meaningful confrontations occur in art. And I shall now take up again the question of thought in relation to violence.

6

THOUGHT

In chapter 3 I was concerned to attack a particular view of the relationship between violence and thought, as manifested in a misconception of what the truly daring and revolutionary in art consists of. It is a view that is a vulgarization of some of the formulations one finds in Artaud, such as the one that I quoted about the beneficial action of theatre in revealing 'the lies, the slackness, baseness, and hypocrisy of our world . . .', or the related assertion that 'If the essential theatre is like the plague, it is . . . because like the plague it is the revelation, the bringing forth, the exteriorization of a depth of latent cruelty by means of which all the perverse possibilities of the mind, whether of an individual or a people, are localized' (p. 30). Behind Artaud himself, of course, stands the complex and life-enhancing system of Surrealism, with its confidence that the more candidly man gazes into the depths of himself, the greater will be his capacity for love and communion. I am speaking, however, of a very different kind of emphasis.

Violence, in this view of things, demonstrates the 'real' nature of man, his fundamental disorderliness and will to destruction, his hatred of constraints, his resentment of ideas and ideals and all other artificial constructions. Hence the artist who deals honestly with violence becomes a kind of nose-rubber or mirror-holder, someone rubbing the spectator's nose in the disagreeable, and holding up a mirror in which he can contemplate the essential filthiness, nastiness, and beastliness of mankind, or at least of unregenerate bourgeois mankind. The truest artists from this point of view are ones like Céline, Zola, Burroughs, Selby, Sade, and Genet, or Shakespeare in *Timon of Athens* and *Lear*, or Goya in *Los Caprichos*, or Bacon *passim*. And behind them hover not only some of the Existentialist formulations about the meaninglessness or absurdity of existence, but Sade's reiterated emphasis on the violence and indifference of Nature, and Swift's image of man-as-Yahoo, and even, most succinctly of all, Saint Bernard's characterization of man as 'a sack of dung, the food of worms'. To express reservations about certain kinds of works, therefore, is to reveal one's own intellectual pusillanimity. One cannot, it would seem, bear to face certain philosophical truths about existence. One cannot bear the artist's 'terrifying honesty'.

What I have just presented is a vulgarization of a vulgarization, of course. But most readers, I imagine, will have encountered the attitude I am talking about, and like all vulgarizations it points towards real phenomena, even though getting them wrong. To involve oneself with violence can indeed compel one into thought about oneself and man and society, sometimes very painful and disconcerting thought. Where actual violences are concerned, Pamela Hansford Johnson's record of her reactions to the Brady–Hindley trial in *On Iniquity* bears honest and eloquent witness to this. And one can well understand her feelings when she says: 'It might have been better for me, as an individual, if I had had nothing to do with this case at all. It has left a mark which I think will never quite be eradicated' (p. 137). Furthermore, A. Alvarez seems right enough when he observes in *The Savage God* that 'when an artist holds a mirror up to nature he finds out who and what he is; but the knowledge may change him irredeemably so that he becomes that image'.[1] However, it is clear that some artists can involve themselves with violences, even the most appalling violences, without losing their way or their balance, and that there is nothing in the least inevitable about a Swiftian view of man any more than there is about a Hobbesian view of society. In *Twilight of the Idols*, Nietzsche enquires: 'What does the tragic artist communicate of himself? Is it not precisely the state *without fear* in the face of the fearful and questionable that he is showing?'[2] I shall begin by considering the kind of courage and stamina required of the artist for certain kinds of explorations – explorations corresponding in some measure to the kind of 'nose-rubbing' that I spoke of above.

To begin with, it is easy to see why there should not be many examples to set beside the tortured Christ of Grünewald's *Crucifixion*, or the grey, eviscerated, yet facially still intensely individual cadaver of Rembrandt's *The Anatomy Lesson*, or the closing sequence in Clouzot's *Manon* in which the corpse of the heroine is manhandled for ten minutes through the Palestine sands by her dying lover,[3] or the shotgun suicide and the frenzied mauling of the body by the madman in *Mort à crédit*, or the disembowelling with a bamboo knife in *Harakiri*, or the charred but still individual figures chained to the stake in one of the most painful of Luiken's prints, or Priam's vision of how, after he has been slain, his own dogs will tear open his corpse and lap his blood, or the following passage from Jean Giono's *Le grand troupeau* about the 1914–18 trenches:

Les morts avaient la figure dans la boue, ou bien
ils émergeaient des trous, paisibles, les mains posées
sur le rebord, la tête couchée sur le bras. Les rats

venaient les renifler. Ils sautaient d'un mort à l'autre. Ils choisissaient d'abord les jeunes sans barbes sur les joues. Ils reniflaient la joue puis ils se mettaient en boule et ils commençaient à manger cette chair d'entre le nez et le bouche, puis le bord des lèvres, puis la pomme verte de la joue. De temps en temps ils se passaient la patte dans les moustaches pour se faire propres. Pour les yeux, ils les sortaient à petites coups de griffes, et ils léchaient le trous des paupières, puis ils mordaient dans l'oeil, comme dans un petit oeuf, et ils le mâchaient doucement, la bouche de côté en humant le jus.[4]

Even when no human violator is involved, the artist himself has to become a species of violator in such invasions of the body's sanctity.

And of course things become much worse, and the entailed risks much greater, in a number of instances in which violators *are* involved, such as the surgical flaying of the kidnapped girl's face in *Les yeux sans visage*, or the impaling of a living man on a sharpened tree branch in *Los Desastros de la Guerra*, or the wrenching-off of a dead man's genitals in Zola's *Germinal* and the brandishing of them on the end of a stick as a trophy, or the gouging out of a man's eyeballs and the crushing of one of them underfoot in *King Lear*. Creating the figures who do such things means allowing full play to the darker parts of the mind without fear of what one may unwittingly be revealing about oneself. It is like Lockwood's dream in *Wuthering Heights*, in which his ruthless sawing of the child's wrist against the broken window-pane suddenly reveals a potentiality for cruelty in himself as great as any displayed subsequently by the less cultured characters in the novel. It involves the kind of Sadean acknowledgment that Nietzsche made in *The Genealogy of Morals* when he observed that 'To behold suffering gives pleasure, but to cause another to suffer affords an even greater pleasure' (p. 198) and that 'pleasure is induced by [a creditor's] being able to exercise his power freely upon one who is powerless, by the pleasure of *faire le mal pour le plaisir de le faire*, the pleasure of rape' (p. 196). And it also entails the artist's willingness not to fear where his explorations may be taking him intellectually, such as the condition described at the end of Baudelaire's 'Les sept vieillards':

Vainement ma raison voulait prendre la barre;
La tempête en jouant déroutait ses efforts,
Et mon âme dansait, dansait, vieille gabarre,
Sans mâts, sur une mer monstrueuse et sans bords![5]

It is a liberal illusion that nothing in the world of thought is irrevocable and that one can always go home again if one chooses. The possibility of a permanent loss of one's bearings is testified to unforgettably in Hawthorne's 'Young Goodman Brown', and it can come about more insidiously than in that story, and be just as damaging. 'Whoever fights monsters,' as Nietzsche observes in *Beyond Good and Evil*, 'should see to it that in the process he does not become a monster. And when you look long into an abyss, the abyss also looks into you.'[6] It is worth considering how that change can happen, and seeing more clearly what the danger is.

Craving certainty, the mind constantly looks for a pattern in existence of which it can feel that this is what existence *essentially* is; and since it also yearns for reassurances of its own normality, its own consonance with the natural order of things, it is prone to engage in distortions and adjustments when things don't fit as they should. The most dramatic example of this is Sade's work, in which he constructs an entire metaphysical system in order to legitimate his own sexual proclivities. And part of the fascination of that work lies in his returning over and over again to certain themes, as if, despite the ostensible certitude of his proofs, he continually felt certain counter-arguments building up, and again and again had to demolish them and reinterpret the proffered evidence about the altruism of love, or the legitimacy of compassion, or the pleasures of tenderness. However, the process of distortion can be more subtle. The shock of certain atrocities, and the recognition of certain dreadful possibilities in other people or in oneself[7] is likely to be especially disruptive if one has tended to feel previously that at bottom life is essentially benevolent – that Good always wins out over Evil because of the essential nature of things, that there are magical limits beyond which people won't go, that the innocent and beautiful, the 'sensitive, the considerate and the plucky' of Forster's ideal aristocracy of the spirit,[8] carry with them their own protections and 'have no enemy but age', as someone puts it, and that when atrocities *are* perpetrated it is by people who have either been victims themselves (as in wartime or in the slum-childhood kind of criminality)[9] or who wear very obviously the marks of monstrosity and of their own eventual downfall. And as a result, one may become more and more preoccupied with awfulness and alert for instances of it, while increasingly it is the glimpses of love and beauty and hope that prove the real threats to one's stability, because they draw attention to one's estrangement from one's more hopeful earlier self. And the more these processes go on, the more likely one is to look for and offer philosophical arguments about the essential awfulness of man, the inevitable cruelty of existence, and so on. Some of the dynamics of this process were obviously at work in the career of Céline, even though in his two masterpieces he was too great and honest an artist to go all the way. The consequences for a lesser talent are apparent in Selby's *Last Exit to Brooklyn*, apart from the hold-out in the 'Landsend' section, which is much the best part of the book.

It is necessary, however, to be alert to a paradox here. As the economic success of Céline, and Selby, and Burroughs, and Genet, and a number of other 'black' writers reminds one, society is surprisingly willing to encourage and reward certain kinds of unpleasantness and cynicism, however ostensibly antagonistic the author may be towards the complacent bourgeois consciousness. And one can see why. The vision of the writer, supposedly so unflinching, so devastatingly honest, etc., is usually so patently selective that the reader can identify its limits fairly quickly and then relax. The respectable reader of Selby (as of Zola in his time) can get his thrills in a sort of psychological Bowery or Reeperbahn that has no real connection with his own mode of life, and return home from his slumming trip feeling agreeably reassured about his own decent normality. And at a different social level, the legions of blue-collar American readers of scandal tabloids and crime magazines obviously enjoy being assured of the omnipresence of violence, cynicism, and corruption, since it makes their own decently undramatic lives appear more admirable in the contrast.

What has gone wrong, I think, is that the artist has incorrectly identified the source of the strain involved in his own perception of things, in his sense of life's intellectual cruelty towards *him* and of the fittingness of his subjecting his audience to the same kind of cruelty. By offering his audience a 'position', even if ostensibly a shocking or depressing one, he has provided them at the outset with exactly what wasn't available to himself to begin with, namely a system in which everything fits more or less neatly into place.[10] In contrast, the truly shocking and cruel in art, I suggest, occurs when the artist's gaze has been turned as firmly and in a sense disinterestedly as possible on concrete human behaviour, and when he himself has been shocked by the capacity of people and events to pass violently beyond limits to which he himself has assented. One of the ironies involved in the notion of the outrageous is the endeavour of proponents of it to get outrageousness all on their own side, so that, emancipated and unshockable themselves, they can watch comfortably as other people are outraged in piquant ways. Good art, however, doesn't shock only the bourgeoisie; in some degree it shocks everyone, including the artist. And it is because of the daring and ruthlessness of its interrogations – its intellectual cruelty in Artaud's sense of that term – that distinguished violent art remains genuinely radical however often one returns to it.

The true mental daring and hardihood are those displayed when the artist simultaneously acknowledges the worth of what is being violated and yet presents unflinchingly its violation. And it *hurts* the reader or viewer to be involved in that process and to feel the broader implications of the violation – to feel that in some real measure it is the natural order of things that is being violated. Watkins' *Culloden*, for instance, which is painful enough during and after the actual fighting, seems to me almost unbearable during the part before the fighting when one is confronted in close-up interviews with some of the individual Highlanders who are going to be butchered and whose fates one is powerless to alter. And a comparable effect occurs in one of the most painful passages in literature that I know of, again from Giono's *Le grand troupeau*. The time is August 1914, the men of the Haute–Provence villages have just been conscripted, and the remaining inhabitants of certain of them are appalled by the sudden appearance of an immense flock of sheep that have been driven down from their summer pastures at a savage pace over rough ground. The passage concerns one of the bellwethers:

> C'était un mâle à pompons noirs. Ses deux larges cornes en tourbillons s'enlargissaient comme des branches de chêne. Il avait posé ses cornes sur les dos des moutons, de chaque côté de lui et il faisait porter sa lourde tête; sa tête branchue flottait sur le flot des bêtes comme une souche de chêne sur la Durance d'orage. Il avait du sang caillé sur ses dents et dans ses babines.
>
> Le détour de la route le poussa au bord. Il essaya de porter sa tête tout seul, mais elle le tira vers la terre, il lutta des genoux de devant, puis s'agenouilla. Sa tête était là, posée sur le sol comme une chose morte. Il lutta des jambes de derrière, enfin il tomba dans la poussière, comme un tas de laine coupée. Il écarta ses cuisses à petits coups douloureux: il avait tout l'entre-cuisse comme une boue de sang avec, là-dedans, des mouches et des abeilles qui bougaient et deux oeufs rouges qui ne tenaient plus au ventre que par un nerf gros comme une ficelle.[11]

Not only have the sheep been hideously over-driven in a violation of all normal husbandry; the episode also brings to mind analogous sufferings possible for the men who have just been herded off to war, and, as with *Culloden*, one becomes conscious of how the decencies of a whole culture are being violated. In *Moby Dick*, similarly, the kind of aggression embodied in the whaling profession in general, the *Pequod* and its mates more specifically, and Ahab above all, is 'placed' by the account in chapter 86 of the Grand Armada of whales quietly going about their underwater domestic lives – innocently sentient beings who may all too easily be reduced to the state of the horribly wounded whale described in the same chapter. And if the death of Hector and the indignities inflicted on his corpse by the vengeful Achilles are as painful as they are, this is substantially because of the beautiful domestic episode earlier in which he and his wife tenderly bid farewell to each other and his baby son is scared by the immense crest of his helmet. The fact that it is when various other heroic figures are going to their deaths – Hamlet, say, or Cassandra – that one is the most aware of their rich identities is also well known. Here, too, patterns of natural rightness and decency, and images of noble potentialities, are exposed in their vulnerability, and then destroyed.

It is examples like these that bring to mind most appropriately some of Artaud's observations about cruelty such as the famous remark that '"*Theatre of cruelty*" means a theatre difficult and cruel for myself first of all' (p. 79), or, 'From the point of view of the mind, cruelty signifies rigor, implacable intention and decision, irreversible and absolute determination. . . . Cruelty is above all lucid . . .' (pp. 101–2), or, 'It is not at all a matter of vicious cruelty, cruelty bursting with perverse appetites and expressing itself in bloody gestures, sickly excrescences upon an already contaminated flesh, but on the contrary, a pure and detached feeling, a veritable movement of the mind based on the gestures of life itself . . .' (pp. 113–14).[12] And the bearing of what I have been saying on the question of censorship should be noted at this point.

It is perfectly true that it is often the horrors that *aren't* shown that are the most disturbing. The mutilated Thing beating on the door in W. W. Jacobs' 'The Monkey's Paw', the silhouettes of the torturers and their implements at the end of James Elroy Flecker's *Hassan*, the torturing of the leper with red-hot shotgun barrels in Kipling's 'The Mark of the Beast' ('Strickland shaded his eyes with his hands for a moment and we got to work. This part is not to be printed'), and so on – if this sort of thing is part of the stock-in-trade of flesh-creeping it is obviously not because of any residual neoclassical sense of decorum on the part of writers and movie-makers but because, as Poe taught everyone with his pit in 'The Pit and the Pendulum', the fascination of the unspeakable or indescribable or unprintable is that the reader always assumes that, whatever it is, it must be worse than the worst that he himself can imagine. Moreover, the unshown sometimes involves an expressive indeterminacy in one's time-sense that is hard to obtain by conventional narration or depiction. In Grosz's 'After the Interrogation',[13] for example, with its glimpsed boots of the S.A. men leaving the cellar on the floor of which lie an overturned stool, a bucket, a pair of suspenders, a broken pair of glasses, and other detritus, the beatings and degradations extend backwards in one's imagination in a way that couldn't have happened had a particular moment of the interrogation been frozen for us. And contrariwise, when in *Nuit et brouillard*, after having had numerous details of camp existence given to us, we are shown virtually without comment, the exterior of the punishment block, it is as if we ourselves had been led up to it and to an infinity of unpredictable torments stretching ahead of us. (A similar effect occurs near the end of *One Day in the Life of Ivan Denisovich* when the Captain is taken off to suffer his ten days in the unheated cells.) It is also true that curiously little awareness has been shown of the fact that Sade pointed to when he asserted in *Les cent vingt jours de Sodome* that the greatest *frissons* often come from hearing someone *recount* outrageousnesses. It may be, of course, that this technique is too disturbing to use much. Viewers of Ophuls' *Le chagrin et la pitié* will no doubt recollect the gasp that went up when a lawyer mentioned four young members of the collaborationist militia having been tried immediately after the Liberation for having gouged out the eyes of two prisoners and then sewn their eyelids shut after putting live cockroaches in the empty sockets, and the chill that descended when a former member of the Resistance spoke briefly of the torture-killing of his wife. And the anonymous *Winter Soldier*, in which former American G.I.s recall atrocities committed by them and others in Vietnam, has been described by a reviewer in *Positif* (Juillet–Août, 1972) as 'one of the most unbearable documents on a war that we have ever seen' (p. 56).

Nevertheless, it is also clear that the kind of cruelty on the artist's part that I have been speaking of is only possible if those magic safeguards that I spoke of earlier aren't present. Describing the experience of viewing Lewis's Grand Guignolesque *Blood Feast*, Michel Caen observed that 'One is very afraid. The morbid dread induced by the film comes from the fact that the normal limits of visual horror are surpassed and that one must be ready for anything. It is impossible to tell at what moment a sequence is going to end.'[14] It isn't necessary for limits to *keep* being passed in a work: the dreadful burning of the old woman at the outset of Dreyer's *Day of Wrath*, for instance, was quite enough to establish the climate of fear in the movie and the implications of being accused of witchcraft at that time. And just as an obvious pattern of Grand Guignol escalation in a work would help the reader to disengage himself from it emotionally, so too the technique of the initial shock can itself become a cliché. In *The Godfather*, for example, the severed head of the racehorse in the movie producer's bed, effective as it was, seemed a little too obviously indebted to the slaughtering of the old gray horse near the opening of *Le sang des bêtes*. But, as I have said before, some shocks *stay* shocking, like Franju's, and are deeply charged with meaning. And to constrain an artist within standards of 'acceptability' may be to damage his work as much as the elimination of every reference to blood ('Yet who would have thought the old man to have had so much blood in him?') would have damaged *Macbeth*.[15] Forbes' movie of life in a Japanese prisoner-of-war camp, *King Rat*, for example, suffered from the coyness with which a vital element in it, the inmates' 'execution' of suspected thieves and traitors by thrusting them head-down into latrine pits, was handled. And a filming of Zola's *L'Assommoir* would be seriously incomplete without the delirium tremens of Coupeau in the Sainte-Anne asylum, or the death of old Bru from starvation in the cubbyhole under the stairs, or the frightful mistreatment of little Lalie by her drunken father. I am talking, naturally, of the kind of treatment in which those horrors are seen as part of the whole structure of meaning of Zola's novel. And this brings me back again to the question of thought.

Speaking of the creative process, Nietzsche observes in *Twilight of the Idols* that:

> What is essential . . . is the feeling of increased strength and fullness. Out of this feeling one lends to things, one *forces* them to accept from us, one violates them — this process is called *idealizing*. Let us get rid of a prejudice here: idealizing does not consist, as is commonly held, in subtracting or

discounting the petty and inconsequential. What is
decisive is rather a tremendous drive to bring out
the main features so that the others disappear in the
process.[16]

In the right kinds of violence, the artist can give back
to thought the kind of existential fulness that is normally
denied to it by the wrong kind of idealizing and abstract-
ing. In some of the most distinguished thinking, of course
– Freud's, for example, or Kierkegaard's, or F. R. Leavis's,
or Nietzsche's own – one has a powerful sense of intensely
individual minds rigorously engaged with reality, including social realities, and of the daring that is involved in
the naked confrontation of adversaries, with reputation,
friendships, social position, employment, all at risk. But
equally obviously, as the various modes of abstraction
and dehumanization testify – bureaucratic, 'technologico-
Benthamite' (Leavis's phrase), McLuhanite, and so on –
the mind is all too vulnerable to seduction by any mode
of thinking, or any intellectual position or strategy, that
permits one to feel a cost-free superiority to others. A fair
amount of what passes for intellection is like this, whether
ostensibly 'committed' (as in the Leftish rhetoric attacked
by Orwell in 'Politics and the English Language') or concerned to avoid commitment (as in the position-switching
that goes on in McLuhan's dodging back and forth between being the one true perceiver among the blind and
being a mere avuncular thrower-out of suggestions, a
modest organizer of probes). And as writers like Sartre
and Camus reminded us, speaking out of their experience
of the Occupation, intellectual positions, ideas, and
value-systems are sometimes only fully vitalized and
assessable when they issue in action, especially action
with grave potential or actual consequences.

In *The Warriors*, Glenn Gray recalled that part of the

appeal of battle is that 'for most soldiers there is the hovering inescapable sense of irreversibility' (pp. 43–4). An essential element in the greatness of Shakespeare's major histories and tragedies is obviously the speeding-up of the processes by which ideologies issue in physical actions of the most irreversible and often shocking kinds. And obviously, too, the decline of British drama during the seventeenth century was partly due to a turning-away from this embodying and testing-out of ideas.[17] It is noteworthy that the English Civil War never got treated dramatically at all and that in the only large-scale work of the period that touched on it even obliquely, namely *Paradise Lost*, the polarizations were in terms not of discussible and intelligent major ideologies but simply of individual vanities – Satan's and God's. The general exhausted turning-away from a contemplation of ideological conflicts was understandable, of course. But the resulting domination of a single version of what reasonableness in politics and philosophy looked like did harm that was by no means entirely rectified later by the idiosyncratic protests of the Romantics. In the States, in contrast, some of the major ideological disagreements that began in the seventeenth century stayed alive into the nineteenth and beyond, issuing not only in the Civil War but in works like *The Scarlet Letter* and *Moby Dick*. And a source of the enduring power of the Western is that it too has permitted the exploration of important conflicts leading to weighty physical confrontations – legality versus the individualism of smallholders; the progressiveness of sheepmen versus the conservatism of cattlemen, and so on – conflicts that in one form or another are still going on in America at large. In works of this sort, one is at a great distance from the kind of discussion drama of Shaw, or Genet, or Weiss in *Marat/ Sade*, in which people merely exchange or juggle ideas.

The protagonists may express ideas, but they are also engaged in enacting them, as they are in works like *War and Peace*, Franz Werfel's *The Forty Days of Musa Dagh*, and the major Greek tragedies. In Artaud's words they are 'men battling hand to hand, bearing within themselves, like stigmata, the most opposed ideas' (p. 127).

Furthermore, as a number of examples that I have already given remind us, part of the seriousness in violent conflicts comes from the convincing representativeness of the violent characters. In children's cartoons, such as The Lone Ranger, the bad guys always loose and are ridiculous into the bargain. In the world of the tougher fairy tales, in contrast, the ogres and wicked stepmothers and murderous kings have plenty of successes to their credit, and even when some of them are brought to justice there will always be others to take their places. Similarly, in some of the fights in the tougher thrillers, such as McPartland's *Face of Evil* and Millar's *Blue City*, not only does it take great skill and strength for the heroes to win, but the losers remain in the mind as frightening presences whose wills are turned implacably against their vanquishers and who with a little more luck might very well have won, so that to attempt to administer private justice against men of this sort would be a very risky business. And what stands out in a number of representative men of violence, whether a smiling murderous bar-room brawler like McPartland's King McCarthy, or Twain's Sherburn, or Achilles coolly putting to death a dozen Trojan prisoners to avenge Patroclus' death, is the completeness of their commitment to courses of violence from which there can be no retreating and in which others may legitimately be no less violent towards them.

It is the entailed revelation of absolutely unbridgeable

differences – of the absolute unshakeableness with which ideas or value-systems that one considers wicked or foolish can be held – that at bottom is so disquieting and challenging about the violences of such men. And what especially disturbs the liberal viewer or reader is the kind of mentality for which destruction – deliberate destruction, with a full knowledge of what is being destroyed – appears perfectly right and natural. One of the most memorably shocking things in Watkins' *Culloden*, for example, was the implacably revenge-seeking Lowlands officer explaining quietly to the interviewer that the atrocities being perpetrated after the battle were *meant* to be atrocious, that the rebellious Highlanders were *meant* to be crushed for ever. It was easy enough for the dismayed liberal viewer to judge him wrong, of course. But one had the disquieting sense not only that there was some show of reason on his side, but that this monstrous behaviour was occurring within the normal framework of his own society, and that in order to argue with him one would have to confront him as a normal social being and not as a monster. Moreover, a great deal of energy and concentration would obviously be required for such a confrontation, and the likelihood of converting him to one's own more civilized value system would be almost nil.[18] This sensed presence of thought behind violence, of violences as manifestations of thought, has further consequences and ramifications.

It is substantially this, I believe, that is responsible for the turnaround that I mentioned earlier in this chapter. When I spoke of the sense of life as being essentially benevolent, what I was pointing to was the belief that certain kinds of tenderness, of lovingness, of harmoniousness and cooperativeness, are so obviously desirable that, given a decent chance to see them, people can't fail to desire them, so that their eventual triumph is assured.

When atrocities occur that don't fit this pattern – when an Edmund or a death-camp torturer, for example, obviously enjoys life more than one does oneself and feels not a scrap of remorse for his actions – the strain to one's metaphysical system can be considerable, in that, as with a figure like Julien, one becomes conscious of one's powerlessness to influence one's imagined opponent in any way. And with the naturalness of one's beliefs brought into question, one may become increasingly fascinated by awfulness, because the more normal it can be made to appear, the less obligation one need feel to be shocked by it and try to combat it. However, it also seems to me that the turnaround would not come about so easily were not a further and more insidious kind of strain often involved. And I would like to return, for the last time, to the question of torture, both because in itself it is the supreme manifestation of the will towards injury, and because it lies at the centre of our perception of Nazism, the most disturbing large-scale display of that will.

Torture is in one respect a little like what used to be described as 'unmentionable' sexual practices: that is, it is something that everyone is aware of, but which one hesitates to speak of dispassionately, for fear that to do so would seem to validate its existence. It has figured more or less prominently in a good many respectable works, however, among them Sartre's *Morts sans sépultures*, Kafka's 'In the Penal Colony', Conrad's *Nostromo*, Koestler's *Darkness at Noon*, Dreyer's *La passion de Jeanne d'Arc*, Goya's *Los desastros de la guerra*, Malraux's *La condition humaine*, Orwell's *Nineteen Eighty-Four*, Foxe's *Book of Martyrs*, and innumerable graphic equivalents of some of the things described in that book. It figures too in a lot of thrillers, including some of the best by Hamilton, Hall, Millar, Ambler, Household,

O'Donnell, and MacDonald, and in the kinds of nine-teenth-century historical novels, such as Ainsworth's, Dumas', and Conan Doyle's, that used to be considered such wholesome reading for boys. The fact that the bulk of the works that I have referred to are works of enter-tainment does not in the least diminish the degree to which they sensitize people to the subject and make them more alert to real-life instances of it. And of course the supreme religious symbol in the Western world is the in-strument of a singularly horrible form of torture killing.[19]

What is more to my purpose here is that the question of torture is more complex than is sometimes allowed for, not only in liberal thinking but in the ostensible anti-thesis of liberal thinking, namely Sade's.

Some torturing, such as that by a number of Sade's monsters, or by such real-life monsters as Erzsébet Báthory or Neville Heath is patently compulsive and mindless. Some, as in the general savagery of savage wars, comes from an uncomplicated lust for revenge, a sentiment whose force, as Nietzsche reminds us, should not be underestimated. Some is purely practical, being thought to be the only way of obtaining important in-formation. (Part of the distinction of Pontecorvo's *The Battle of Algiers*, for example, was the lucidity with which the Massu-surrogate French colonel was permit-ted to present the question in this light to the assembled journalists.[20]) And some has certain quasi-philosophical overtones. Sartre's statement in *What is Literature?* that the torturer 'has, in a single victim, symbolically gratified his hatred of all mankind' (p. 161) was obviously true of a number of figures at work in Europe during the Second World War. And that kind of hatred, that will to domina-tion, can, when becoming somewhat more specialized, as in a figure like Ezzelino da Romano, or some of the other Sadean figures that I have mentioned, become the sort of thing that Sade was increasingly preoccupied with in *Juliette*: that is, an almost cosmic will to dominance, an obsessive assertion of the isolated, unreachable self against all that is organic and natural, all natural pieties and connections, all claims of any kind that can be made upon the individual in the name of the more than merely individual. However, it is obvious that a good deal of torturing is charged with thought, imbued with thought, inseparable from thought, in a simpler and more disturbing fashion.

What Bertrand Russell in *Power* called '"naked" power, i.e. . . . the kind that involves no acquiescence on the part of the subject',[21] seems relatively uncommon. What is far more common is what Koestler explored in *Darkness at Noon* and what increasingly preoccupied Orwell, namely the will towards producing a lasting acquiescence, an ultimately voluntary submission. Even the kind of brutality displayed in *The Brig* or in the stockade section of James Jones' *From Here to Eternity*, like the para-military structure of the pre-war concentration camps, is chiefly aimed at breaking down and restructuring the minds of those undergoing it. And this compulsion can manifest itself equally in Spanish inquisitors, in Stalinist interrogators, in Chinese brainwashers in North Korea, in French torturers in Algeria, in the Algerian torturers who succeeded them,[22] in the torturers of the Colonels' Greece, in the Soviet psychiatrists who have infamously lent themselves to the shock-treatment of intellectual dissenters in recent years, and in the kinds of mental health specialists in England and the States who would be only too happy to be given a completely free hand to 'cure' social deviants of one kind or another.[23] In part, no doubt, this is simply a more subtle form of the will to dominate, resulting in Sadean gratifications of a sort that Sade himself never understood. Part of the paradox of Sade's works, namely the constant escalation of the crimes in an ever-unsuccessful attempt to arrive at crimes that will be *truly* shocking and truly gratifying to those committing them, stems from the fact that there is no will towards conversion in their perpetrators, and hence no genuine struggle the outcome of which, as each new persecution and martyrdom is embarked upon, must always of necessity remain in doubt until the full yielding has occurred. Like their tormentors, Sade's more virtuous victims, such as Justine, Madame de Mistival in *La philosophie dans le boudoir*, and Constance in *Les cent vingt jours de Sodome*, simply persist unchanged in their convictions. But clearly more is usually involved in what I am talking about than the very real pleasure of breaking someone down and in a sense remaking him or her.

At times, no doubt, there is a genuine desire to improve or save someone 'for his own good'. The activities of a good many inquisitors, penologists, schoolmasters, mental health experts and so on, are presumably explicable in this way. And clearly some of the more odious activities of the French army in Algeria derived from the conviction that the moral realities of 'civilized' French order were so patently good and desirable that a lasting peace would quickly result if the army could only deal incisively enough with the presumed handful of hard-core 'agents' and 'agitators'.[24] But there is often something else involved, I believe. Speaking of the concentration camps, David Rousset observed in *L'Univers concentrationnaire* that:

> The purpose of the camps is indeed physical
> destruction, but the actual aim of the
> concentrationary universe goes far beyond all this.
> The SS does not conceive of his adversary as a

normal man. The enemy, according to the philosophy of the SS, is the physical and intellectual embodiment of the Power of Evil. . . . Death therefore is not enough. Only expiation can assuage and soothe the Master Race. The concentration camps are an amazing and complex mechanism of expiation. [*The Other Kingdom*, p. 109].

The threat posed when the individual's resistance testifies to the sustaining power of his ideology can be considerable. And it is the almost metaphysical dread aroused by such a perception – the feeling that if the antagonist can really live unshakeably in a universe so fundamentally different from what one conceives the universe to be, then one's own conception may be fundamentally wrong, all one's values constructed on sand, and all one's passions in support of them fundamentally absurd – that is responsible for the especial bitterness of civil wars and for the related horror and rage often inspired by the figure of the heretic.[25] Moreover, this feeling seems to me more widespread than is commonly allowed for.

Writing of the Brady–Hindley trial, Pamela Hansford Johnson observed that 'It is a peculiar fact that whenever there was a stir in the court-room at all . . . this was not in response to some horror, but rather, to some more than commonly callous or preposterous lie' (pp. 71–2), and said of the courtroom spectators that 'They wanted to see someone break [Hindley] down. I wanted to see it myself. This was partly a vengeful feeling, and partly the feeling of sheer frustration at being unable to understand what was going on behind that pink and white mask' (pp. 97–8). Much the same feelings, I take it, were aroused in a good many of us by those photographs of the radiant-looking young girls in their summer dresses in the Manson trial and by the reports of them laughing and twittering together in the courtroom. So too with Nazism. 'For years to come,' reported Gerald Reitlinger of the post-1945 years in *The SS, Alibi of a Nation*, 'the hard-core SS in captivity were the despair of liberal-minded persons who tried to re-educate them in accordance with democratic dogma.'[26] And faced with the chuckling former S.S. men on trial in Weiss's *The Interrogation*, one feels a craving for anything, almost anything, that would break them down; for violations, even, in which the fury of the violators might bear compelling witness to the abhorrence in which their actions were held. It is noteworthy that *Othello* ends with the promised torturing of Iago, and that the notion of torture in this connection is very different from the Grand Guignol torture-killing of Edward II in Marlowe's play of that name. Shakespeare displayed in at least three other works – *Richard III, King Lear*, and *The Tempest* – his concern with the unreachable and utterly unrepentant semi-philosophical murderer, the more or less Sadean figure. In the promised torturing of Iago, it is as if he were simultaneously acknowledging the craving to close a kind of metaphysical gap through the coerced acknowledgment of error by a representative 'Sadean' figure, and at the same time, in Iago's convincing 'Demand me nothing: what you know, you know;/From this time forth I never will speak more,' conceding the unlikelihood of being able to do so.

Hence part of the strain of trying to cope, if only intellectually and at several removes, with perpetrators of violences that shock one is that the more intensely one feels, and the more one thinks in terms of counter-action oneself, the more one is liable to find oneself being edged logically towards an acknowledgment of the strength of the will to dominate – and hence towards a kind of unwilling underpinning of at least part of the

Weltanschauung of those whose activities one so much detests. And this fact of the will to domination, if only moral or intellectual domination, seems to me to have certain bearings on the question of the revolutionary in art.

7

RESPONSIBILITIES

One of the commonest revolutionary illusions, especially during the 1960s, has been that the rottenness of society is evidence of its vulnerability. The informing metaphor or analogy is presumably that of the sturdy-seeming tree that has become hollow inside and can be toppled by a casual storm or a few resolute strokes of the axe. And a related belief is that it is only necessary to point to the more patently ludicrous or shocking aspects of official behaviour – often shocking *because* ludicrous – for the rottenness of the whole system to become apparent to everyone. This seems to me to be getting things the wrong way round.

The actual inhumanities in institutional medicine, law-enforcement, the administration of justice, and so on are indeed frequently more grotesque than those examples that Burroughs displays to us in *Naked Lunch* or that Joseph Heller shows in *Catch-22*. The sanity of society, as works like Franju's *La tête contre les murs* and Wiseman's *The Titicutt Follies* remind us, may be madder at times than the madness that it condemns to incarceration. Its 'legality', as in the guillotining at the end of Becker's *Le casque d'or*, or in parts of Lelouch's *La vie, l'amour, la mort*, may be more dreadful than some of the crimes that it punishes. And how moderate our movie-makers have really been in their protests – or, perhaps more accurately, have been *permitted* to be – can perhaps be gauged from the unlikelihood of any movie-maker's being able to make a ruthlessly realistic use of the incident described in a mid-nineteenth century letter which Alvarez quotes in *The Savage God*:

> Two young girls in Chelsea have died of hunger. They were so thin that there was no flesh on their bones and their skin was of a greenish colour. A man was hanged who had cut his throat, but who had been brought back to life. They hanged him for suicide. The doctor had warned them that it was impossible to hang him as the throat would burst open and he would breathe through the aperture. They did not listen to his advice and hanged their man. The wound in the neck immediately opened and the man came back to life again although he was hanged. It took time to convoke the aldermen [*sic*] to decide the question of what was to be done. At length the aldermen assembled and bound up the neck below the wound *until he died* (p. 336).[1]

There are large-scale examples too. What made the French torturing in Algeria so shocking was not simply the activity itself, just as the most shocking thing about the Dreyfus affair was not just that an innocent man had been imprisoned. What was also shocking was the official hypocrisy, whitewashing, and brazen lying, and the fact that the whole anti-torture campaign in France was conducted, in Pierre Vidal-Naquet's words, 'with negligible results'.[2] And the same plainly holds true of a lot of American governmental behaviour concerning Vietnam.

But in contrast to the use of naked unapologetic force, as by the Tontons Macoutes of François Duvalier's Haiti or in the Odessa Steps massacre in Eisenstein's *Battleship Potemkin*, such things often testify, I fear, not to the rottenness of a social structure but to its strength. For what faces one in the passage about the hanging is what also faces one in the fact that the two Dominican authors of the fifteenth-century *Malleus Maleficarum* could earnestly insist that when a suspected witch was racked on two separate days, she was not, strictly speaking, being tortured twice, since

> We do not intend to use the rack a second time;
> far be it from us to do this without fresh and weighty
> reasons; we are only going to continue the process
> another day. We are well aware that it would be
> contrary to justice and reason to repeat the trial by
> torture. God preserve us from being so inhuman and
> cruel, we only intend to postpone further
> proceedings for another time. . . .[3]

And one sees the same sort of thing in the fact that in 1955 the civil Inspector General Roger Wuillaume, having lucidly reported his official findings about the actualities of torture in Algeria that the authorities had been trying to cover up, should still have been able to recommend to the Paris government that:

> It goes without saying that all physical violence
> verging upon torture must be prohibited. . . . On
> the other hand the water and electricity methods,
> provided they are carefully used, are said to produce
> a shock which is more psychological than physical
> and therefore does not constitute excessive
> cruelty. . . . I am inclined to think that these
> procedures can be accepted and that, if used in the
> controlled manner described to me, they are no
> more brutal than deprivation of food, drink, and
> tobacco, which has always been accepted.[4]

What such passages reveal helps to explain the enduring power of bureaucratic-authoritarian structures, namely the ability of men of intelligence and goodwill to believe that authority must maintain itself at any cost in the interests of 'order', and to adjust their moral perceptions accordingly so that the atrocious comes to seem perfectly reasonable and even beneficent.

If this can occur where the patently outrageous, the ludicrously untrue or self-contradictory is concerned, the bureaucratic-authoritarian mind can obviously function with even more self-assurance where less dramatic but more widespread injustices and absurdities are concerned.[5] This kind of inertia, with all its obduracy and resiliency, is probably one of the hardest things for would-be revolutionaries to contemplate unflinchingly. There is obviously a fear that to look too squarely at the facts would entail despair about significant improvements ever coming about, and hence a failure to engage in the very activities that might make for change. The collapse of the student radical movement in America at the end of the 1960s indicates that the fear was not groundless.

And the bearing on the question of revolutionary art of what I have been saying so far will probably be fairly clear by now. If genuine protest art – in which category I include such diverse works as *The Death Ship*, *A Day in the Life of Ivan Denisovich*, *L'Univers concentrationnaire*, *Punishment Park*, *Los Desastros de la Guerra*, *La tête contre les murs*, *The Exterminating Angel*, *Zéro de conduite*, and *Nuit et brouillard* – is to be truly effective, it must, I think, answer to the requirements made in the passage quoted earlier from *Anatomy of the SS State* about the 'sleepy conscience'.[6] That is to say, what is under attack must be grasped as firmly and solidly as possible, which in turn means that it must have been observed precisely and in some real measure understood from the inside. Caricature and grotesquerie may serve in a rough fashion in the task of identifying and de-sanctifying enemies, but their effect is all too likely to wear off with the passing of time, unless the caricaturist is, like Daumier, a very intelligent and accurate observer. Burroughs' social criticisms in *Naked Lunch*, for instance, seem to me clear examples of the wrong kind of 'idealization' in Nietzsche's sense of the term: the author has simply abstracted prematurely the idea of a callous surgeon or police-state official or obnoxious plutocrat in such a way that it doesn't epitomize but lies to one side of the actualities. And the same can be said of the ostensibly energetic protests of the 'MacSpaunday' group in the 1930s, such as Auden and Isherwood's *The Dog beneath the Skin* or Stephen Spender's *Trial of a Judge*, and of recent American protest plays like Barbara Garson's vulgar *MacBird*. It can be added that the distrust which the MacSpaunday group aroused at the time in the *Scrutiny* critics received confirmation not only from their failure to fight in the Spanish Civil War but from their not having seen active service in World War Two; those facts, I mean, reflected back damagingly on the quality of their anti-Fascism and their emphasis on political 'commitment', and probably bore some relationship to the general meretriciousness of their styles. Significantly, it was not Auden but Orwell – who, almost uniquely among his literary contemporaries, had known violence at first-hand and fought in Spain – who became the conscience of his generation.[7]

Protest of the right kind doesn't need to be solemn, of course. In much of the best movie comedy, the bogus in society gets shown up as what it is – sets of conventions which normally make it easier to control and exploit people, but which, if challenged forcibly enough, can be turned against their proponents. But the lasting power of the great comic figures when they are at their best lies nonetheless in their demonic self-assertions being made against very concretely rendered and often counter-active social institutions. I am thinking above all of Chaplin here, particularly in works like that greatest of all comic shorts, *The Cure*. But Coulteray's observation that 'the chief virtue of Chaplinesque cruelty . . . is that it is total. It respects absolutely nothing'[8] also applies to the Marx Brothers (particularly in *Animal Crackers* and *A Night at the Opera*), Laurel and Hardy in movies like *Two Tars, Men o' War*, and *Battle of the Century*, and at times W. C. Fields. And a common feature of the weaker comedians, such as Harold Lloyd, Abbot and Costello, and the Three Stooges, is that either their energies are turned chiefly against themselves or else, if they *do* cause social disruptions of one kind or another, it is to a large extent inadvertently, and often with embarrassment. In the works of the latter group, bourgeois decencies and decorums go essentially unquestioned; indeed, they are even indirectly bolstered up by the characters' embarrassment and by the unanalytical conventionality with which they are presented. In the best works of the former, and in a masterpiece like Clair's *Italian Straw Hat*, they are unmistakably the enemy; and implicit in the irreverence is a diagnostic approach to such things as the display rites of the *nouveaux riches*, the predatory activities of employers, the at times stifling atmosphere of small-town life and of money-oriented lower-middle-class marriages, and the protective–oppressive institutions of police and judiciary in a booming capitalistic society. It is hardly surprising that Chaplin's influence should have been so considerable in works like *Voyage au bout de la nuit, The Death Ship, Zéro de conduite*, and *The Horse's Mouth*.

As I said, however, a crucial factor in the right kind of protest art is an understanding of what is being attacked. And part of that understanding is the ability to see both the ridiculous or evil aspects of the institutions under attack and their strengths – that is, not to reduce them, for the sake of propaganda or of one's peace of mind, to the merely ludicrous or grotesque. After all, it is partly the real strengths of various social structures that give them moral self-assurance. Involved in the bureau-cratic-authoritarian attitude there is obviously a deep dread of anything resembling 'disorder', whether in the psyche, or in institutions, or in society at large. And be-yond a certain point of liberalization, the dread can increase so sharply that almost any sanctions against those who appear to be promoting disorder start to appear justifiable. It seems necessary, therefore, for would-be revolutionary or radical artists not to be con-fused or hypocritical about certain aspects of social structures.

In the mid-1960s, Christopher Lasch observed in *Commentary* that, 'As so often happens in American radicalism, power and authority themselves are defined as the source of evil.'[9] But part of the strength of authority lies in what Orwell recognized and drew attention to again and again, namely that its vision of reality (or at least of *Realpolitik*) does correspond to certain actualities, as a movie like *Le sang des bêtes* reminds us. As one watches that movie for the first time, one is liable to feel an appalled and steadily intensifying sympathy for the butchered animals, and to accompany this with a progressive dehumanizing of the slaughterers: a period photograph of one of them evokes patronizing laughter, the news that another of them lost a leg through wielding his skinning-knife care-lessly is liable to provoke the reaction, 'Serve the brute right!' And then a casual and unironical reference is made in the commentary to 'this difficult and dangerous métier', and one realizes what one has been up to. There is a common tendency to turn off one's imagination at certain points and refuse to contemplate the possibility of having to do certain things and cope with the attendant moral problems. The things simply get done by the social machine, and one can keep one's clear conscience and one's moral indignation unsullied. But Franju's slaughterers, and others like them elsewhere, *are* taking risks, and they are taking them on our behalf because most of us enjoy eating meat and would be too squeamish or incompetent to do the butchering ourselves. And among the merits of certain violent and irreversible situations is that they can bring one to a point beyond which certain options cannot continue to remain open and a choice must be made.[10] Faced with Franju's brilliant movie, one may decide to stop eating meat, or one may conclude regretfully that, as Gabriel Vialle puts it, 'this nightmare . . . is nothing other than the objective vision of a daily reality, unavoidable, necessary, and vital . . .,'[11] but one cannot logically both feel superior to the slaughterers and go on enjoying roast lamb and *côte de veau*. And the same holds true of more complex and ambiguous situations and problems. One of the most bogus attitudes of all is that of the kind of libertarian who is vehemently against the constraints of society *tout court*, while at the same time taking full advantage of the securities that his or her particular society provides. And art provides us with reminders of its bogusness.

This is at its most apparent where the question of crime is concerned, or at least of certain kinds of crime. It can be presumed that a number of people would still agree with Auden's remark in the mid-1930s that 'Every educated middle-class man (or woman) really knows [it] to be true . . . that violence is always and unequivocally bad. No personal experience, no scientific knowledge, gives any other verdict than that what you can self-forgetfully love, you can cure.'[12] And it is obvious that the instinctive reaction of many people during the past few years has been that in any clash the police must inevitably be in the wrong simply because they *are* police. It seems to me to be a good thing to be reminded as sharply as possible of the existence of violent men who are entirely unconcerned as to whether one loves them or not, and of what the consequences in specific situations are likely to be if no violence can be used against them. Unpleasant as the police can no doubt be – and the fiction even of sympathetic observers of police procedures and routines like Ed McBain, Hillary Waugh, and Chester Himes in the States, and Maurice Procter, Douglas Warner, James Barlowe, and Alan Prior in England, not to mention movies like *The French Connection*, is disquieting enough at times[13] – and symbiotic as the relationship between police and professional criminals no doubt often is, one can still feel profoundly thankful not to live in a society in which free rein is given to the convincingly odious professional criminals of various kinds that one encounters in movies like *On the Waterfront*, *Kiss Me Deadly*, *The Enforcer*, Cammell and Roeg's *Performance*, and the thrillers of McPartland and MacDonald.[14]

In this connection, some of the situations I spoke of in my second chapter are of particular interest. I am referring to ones in which individuals or groups, deprived of the customary protection offered by police or military, are confronted with potential violations from which the only escape is to become temporarily more cunning and violent than those who menace them. Admittedly such a plot, especially when exploited by women writers,

can be one of the silliest in crime fiction, the isolation being so often patently avoidable. And where ideological
overtones are combined with gross implausibility, as in
Straw Dogs, it can be nasty too. Moreover, on a larger
scale the situation has obviously been susceptible of abuse
in the service of propaganda of one kind or another. Confronted with the missionary compound besieged by the
murderous Masai in Rider Haggard's *Allan Quatermain*,
or the missions and legations beleaguered in China during
the Boxer Rebellion, or the innumerable groups of
settlers behind circled wagons or inside log cabins in
Westerns, it used to be all too easy, at least for the young,
not to question by what right they came to be there in
the first place, and to take at face-value the iniquitous-
ness of the besiegers. But as episodes like the Speck, and
Manson, and *In Cold Blood* killings, and a good many
other reported incidents in the States have demonstrated,
the most disquieting thing about what I called the
'domestic violation' situation is that it actually occurs,
just as Hell's Angels invasions or attempted invasions of
small towns have actually occurred,[15] and just as various
other extreme situations actually occur – which is substantially why they come to be dealt with in art in the
first place. A novel like MacDonald's *The Executioners*
(*Cape Fear* in a later edition), with its relatively scrupu-
lous exploration of the 'invasion' situation, and its dread-
fully convincing psychopath, seems to me genuinely
useful in this connection, and so do the violation movies
that I mentioned in chapter 2, with their reminders that,
as Orwell said in 'Rudyard Kipling', 'men can only be
highly civilized while other men, inevitably less civilized,
are there to guard them'.

The reader or viewer of such works is not obliged to
come down on the side of self-defensive violence. Some
people's pacifism is absolute and heroic, even if, as

Orwell felt about Gandhi, perhaps slightly inhuman. One of the most powerful shorts that I can recall seeing was an anti-war documentary, the climax of which was a long vigil mounted by a line of Quakers around the Pentagon. As the camera studied those sombre, silent, implacable figures, while the military men with their brief-cases passed up and down the steps between them, one had a sense of an almost martial conflict in which, whatever violence was done to them, the protestors would never submit or yield. And at a lower level Wyler's *Friendly Persuasion*, as I recall, dealt in a charming and civilized way with Gary Cooper as a Quaker farmer successfully resisting the provocations to violence given him by marauding Southern soldiers during the Civil War (though it would have been a more serious, if less charming, movie had the soldiers themselves behaved really violently). But Axel Heyst's paralysis of the will in *Victory* is a very different matter. And, like the passivity of the protagonist in the first part of *Straw Dogs*, it is obviously partly the result of a failure to have thought clearly about the nature of social order in a way that prepares one to face a variety of eventualities, including the violence of others.

This does not mean that there is anything to be said for the kind of politics, or military campaigning, or law-enforcement in which confrontations are seen in terms of challenges to one's *machismo*; and it might have been appropriate if the distaste of French intellectuals for the unfortunate Lyndon Johnson had moderated the at times extravagant French enthusiasm for John Wayne. But if there are limitations to the image of the Western hero grimly taking down his gunbelt from the wall for the final showdown, there are greater ones to that of his nice-but-narrow wife or fiancée hysterically clutching at his gun-arm in blank indifference to the nature of the conflict or the consequences if he backs away from it. It was E. M. Forster, that most civilized of men, who observed in 'What I Believe' (1939):

> While we are trying to be sensitive and advanced and affectionate and tolerant, an unpleasant question pops up: does not all society rest upon force? If a government cannot count upon the police and the army, how can it hope to rule? And if an individual gets knocked on the head or sent to a labour camp, of what significance are his opinions?

And it was Friedrich Engels who remarked in 1873 about a certain class of socialists:

> They demand that the first act of the social revolution shall be the abolition of authority. Have these gentlemen ever seen a revolution? A revolution is certainly the most authoritarian thing there is; it is the act whereby one part of the population imposes its will on the other part by means of rifles, bayonets and cannon – authoritarian means if such there be at all; and if the victorious party does not wish to have fought in vain, it must maintain this rule by means of the terror which its arms inspire in the reactionaries.[16]

It should not be forgotten, either, that two of the greatest works in English literature, *Wuthering Heights* and *The Tempest*, are explorations of closed situations in which no appeal can be made to shared principles or to larger social structures – and that one of the clear morals of both of them is that if intelligent and civilized people are not prepared to exert themselves with the necessary firmness, they will be destroyed or seriously injured by those who are.[17]

Moreover, what I have been saying has its bearings on the American instability with respect to violence that I talked about in chapters 2 and 3. The instability is historically understandable, of course. Much of the strain of American liberalism has plainly come from trying to maintain civilized standards in a country where there has been so much more violence and disorder than in Britain;[18] and the British reviewer who recently referred impatiently to 'the characteristic American belief in human goodness and perfectability, given only the creation of a benign environment"[19] was oversimplifying matters. If such a belief has in fact been held with excessive strength by a lot of people, this has partly been because of the need not to surrender to the counterpoising American tradition of belief in people's innate and irredeemable wickedness. And violences like the Civil War, and the disgraceful treatment of the Indians during the westward expansion,[20] and the strike-breaking of the labour wars, and the Southern lynchings, and the race riots in the early 1940s, and all the other violences since then, have obviously provided considerable reinforcement for that view, or at least enough to nourish the tradition of pessimism that one sees in writers like Hawthorne and Melville, in whose works and lives are displayed certain ominous possibilities for psychic collapse. At the same time, the attempt to cordon off and quarantine violence intellectually seems to me likely, if anything, to increase the likelihood of disgusting violence occurring. It is psychologically convincing that in *Straw Dogs* the hero, when he does finally resolve to act, moves at one bound from an ignoble passivity to a scarcely more creditable viciousness; and a similar excessiveness has been displayed in the official killings at Kent University, and Attica Prison, and in some of the ghetto riots. The two phenomena seem to me related to each other. When the only options are pure non-violence or undiluted violence, it becomes harder for the kinds of intermediate relationships to be worked out that may in fact render violence unnecessary. And by positing too absolute a gap between violent and non-violent states of being, and by viewing men whose occupations may oblige them to engage in violence as scapegoats or pariahs, 'decent' Americans have almost certainly made it harder for them to develop judgment, flexibility, and self-control in the use of it. After all, if one is going to be damned whatever one does, one may as well go the limit and gratify one's natural desire for melodrama. The intellectual stance of a figure like Orwell seems to me not only more sophisticated but more viable and more humane, and in the remainder of this chapter I shall glance briefly at its sources.

The subject of violence, particularly in relation to the problem of power, was one that Orwell returned to again and again, and part of his exemplary strength was that he was able to do so without any reductionism or exclusions. Long before it was modish to complain about 'elitist' cultural attitudes, he himself succeeded in discussing 'low' forms of art without being either a prig or a cultist, and without feeling that to acknowledge one's 'inferior' tastes cast any doubt upon the reality and importance of more consciously arrived-at ones. And just as he could admit to his own real enjoyment, past or present, of works like Kipling's *Barrack Room Ballads* and E. W. Hornung's Raffles books, so also where actual violences were concerned he could take cognizance of his own aggressive attitudes and acknowledge in 'Shooting an Elephant', for example, that 'With one part of my mind I thought of the British Raj as an unbreakable tyranny, as something clamped down, *in saecula saeculorum*, upon the will of prostrate peoples; with another part I thought that the greatest joy in the world would be to drive a bayonet into a Buddhist priest's guts.' The reason for this, I think, was not simply the greater stability of British society, or the precedents set in the exploration of the typology of violence by writers like Shakespeare, Blake, and Emily Brontë, important as those explorations are. It is always possible for a nation to misread its classics, as the reputations of *Wuthering Heights* and of Lawrence's work prior to *Scrutiny* demonstrate, and the pacific tradition in British thought has been a powerful one. One sees it manifesting itself particularly strongly in Dickens' work, where there is something very like the conventional American dichotomy – outrageous violence on the one hand (the private sort in Bill Sykes, the public in the Gordon Riots and the *Tale of Two Cities* bacchanalia), the David Copperfield kind of domestic bliss on the other. And the manipulative Benthamite tradition has also been strong, achieving its political coming-out in the later nineteenth century in the Fabian movement. No, what really made the difference, I believe, was British Imperialism and the late-nineteenth-century apologetics for it, especially those of Kipling. If the craving for violence that Orwell experienced in Burma was a consequence of Imperialism, so too was his ability to speak about it as he did. The nature of Imperialism and imperialist propaganda not only served to legitimate violence in certain respects, but also enriched the conceptualizing of it in ways that didn't occur in America and that need not have occurred in Britain.

As Arendt points out in *The Origins of Totalitarianism*, 'open disregard for law and legal institutions and ideological justification of lawlessness has been much more characteristic of continental than of overseas imperialism' (p. 243). The function of the U.S. Army in relation to the American imperial expansion on the North American continent was primarily one of assisting whites to take over the lands of non-whites, and then protecting them against the desperation and rage induced by a succession of shamelessly disregarded treaties and broken promises; and there was nothing to take pride in in the army's extra-territorial activities in the Phillipines and Cuba. Where British imperialism was concerned, on the other hand (with the exception of Ireland, which is probably why Ireland is so disliked in England), it was not mere propaganda that made it possible to see the judicious use of force as having helped to protect the innocent against a worse use of force by others. The British overseas did indeed by and large do their best to put a stop to various odious and indefensible exploitations, such as the slave-trading in Africa or the sometimes appalling treatment of child-brides in India. And, given the fact of imperial expansion in the first place, what happened in British-occupied territories was obviously preferable to what had been done by the Spanish in Mexico and Peru in the sixteenth century, or was going on in the late nineteenth and early twentieth centuries in King Leopold's *domaine privée* in the Belgian Congo.[21] Insufferable as Kipling may often be (and the attempted academic booming of his stock seems to me a disturbing symptom), his general presentation of British administrators in India, and that of his *vulgarisateur* Edgar Wallace with respect to Africa, appear to have had a good deal of truth to them in at least one very important respect, as numerous memoirs and reminiscences have testified, among them Leonard Woolf's. What counted above all in local administration was not force but intelligence and 'character' – intelligence, self-control, flexibility, an understanding of local morals and mores, and an ability to provide the kind of justice that was *seen* to be reasonably just.[22]

Given this general framework of a reasonable decency

of intent and a respectable measure of accomplishment, it has been easier for British writers to take cognizance of some of the practical complexities involved in the exercise of power. In his essay on Kipling, Orwell pointed out that Kipling 'identified himself with the ruling power and not with the opposition. In a gifted writer this seems to us strange and even disgusting, but it did have the advantage of giving Kipling a certain grip on reality. The ruling power is always faced with the question, "In such and such circumstances, what would you *do*?", whereas the opposition is not obliged to take responsibility or make any real decisions.' And, faced with the obligation to act in the public good rather than for self-aggrandisement or in response to the pressures of political corruption (the latter so American a preoccupation where power is concerned[23]), it has been easier for the decent individual to engage in limited violence without feeling that he has thereby betrayed his own humanity, and for an ethics of violence, a structure of actual or hypothetical test-cases, to be worked out. In this respect Orwell's own debt to Kipling, for all his divergences from him, is obviously great. Again and again in his essays, whether in the situation of 'Shooting an Elephant', or in a statement like, 'In relation to the late [1939–45] war, one question that every pacifist had a clear obligation to answer was: "What about the Jews? Are you prepared to see them exterminated? If not, how do you propose to save them without resorting to war?"', he raises the question of alternatives. There has been correspondingly more room in Britain, as, for example, in the espionage novels of Grahame Greene, Len Deighton, Martin Woodhouse, Simon Harvester, and Adam Hall, for explorations of situations in which appearances are untrustworthy, and no formulae can be applied mechanically, and it is sometimes very difficult to decide which of various alternatives is the least evil, but in which one must choose and act all the same.[24] And there is one other respect in which Kipling's work seems to have counted.

Partly, as I have said, what Kipling did corresponded to the official image of Imperial-oriented organizations, especially the Army and the public-school system with its concern with producing young administrators with the right kind of 'character'. But in works like *Stalky and Co.* and a number of the Indian tales he also opened up a region of violence that was neither purely institutional and systematized (as in Melville's *White Jacket* and *Billy Budd*) nor purely private and anarchic (as in Poe, Bierce, and Twain), and which was different from anything to be found in other nineteenth-century British novelists like Dickens, Gissing, and Hardy. I am speaking of the study of protagonists who are committed to order in principle and are usually themselves members of order-creating organizations, but who pass over the border of the legal and acceptable, whether as the result of a disdain for minor regulations, or a temporary flagging of the will, or a sudden explosion or implosion of anger or fear. H. G. Wells intensified and coarsened this pattern, with more hysterical individual violences on the one hand and a more machine-like ideal of social order and efficiency on the other; Conrad intensified and refined it, with a greater emphasis on implosion and collapse. And even writers like Lawrence, Forster, and Joyce Cary, exploring not only the forces in the psyche making for disorder and destruction but the ways in which they could make for a greater fulness of being and an enriched creativity, were indebted to what Kipling had done.[25] They were obviously in indignant recoil from the narrowness of the Kiplingesque vision of man, of society, of the good life, of relationships between the sexes, and of art. But in their best work they too were

150

always concerned as much with society and the possibility of viable modes of social existence as they were with the explosive self.[26]

Given all this; given too the long and noble tradition of British protest against gratuitous cruelty, whether to children (as in Blake and Dickens) or to animals (as in Hogarth, Blake, Clare, and such anti-vivisectionist writers as Edward Carpenter, H. S. Salt, Frances Power Cobbe, and Bernard Shaw); and given also the scarcely less strong tradition of distrust of the 'strong man' and *Realpolitik* (the favourite British historical figures, after all, are mostly losers, like Bonnie Prince Charlie, or mavericks, like Nelson), it has been easier in Britain to take serious cognizance of violence, and of impulses towards violence in oneself, without feeling that one is thereby moving towards an approval of civic disintegration, or brute force, or a neo-Nietzschean will-to-power, or mere sadism. The subject is still a minefield, however, and by way of conclusion I shall try to make clearer certain attitudes informing the present work.

8

CONCLUDING

In speaking as I did in the previous chapter, I was not, of course, setting up in business as a belated apologist for imperialism. What I was trying to define were certain strengths, a certain breadth and stability, in the attitude towards power and violence that can be called Orwellian and that seems to me about as near to socio-political sanity about those matters as one can hope to get in these increasingly dispiriting times. It is an attitude which, like the *Scrutiny* stance towards culture, is separable from any particular politics but is such that any political position sharply at odds with it deserves to be viewed with caution. And the right kinds of violences in art are not only charged with meaning but serve to block off, or at least make harder, a contrasting attitude. I am referring to the sort of ironical contemplation of the human labyrinth in which one refrains from becoming intensely committed to any single point of view and any long-term course of action, especially political action, because it is too difficult to determine where truth and justice really lie.

This attitude obviously derives in part from the experience of tragedy, particularly Greek tragedy. And faced, say, with the passionate confrontation in Aeschylus' *Agammemnon* between the bloodstained Clytemnestra and the outraged Chorus, with the diatribe of the butchered Cassandra still lingering in our ears, it is easy enough to see its moral attractions. As Gilbert Murray observes, Greek tragedy 'presents us with no villains, no monsters – no one who has not some real point of view for us to understand or, at least, some plausible case for us to consider'.[1] In the *Iliad*, similarly, a sense of the nobility on both sides and the painfulness of its destruction is absolutely central, as it is to a lesser extent in a play like *Henry IV Part I*.[2] So too with a number of actual conflicts. The English Civil War, for example, still offers as rich a subject as the American one to the movie-maker capable of comprehending imaginatively the cultural issues involved, and of seeing the grandeur and pathos of a figure like Cromwell and the countervailing strengths of the England that he was at odds with. And part of the fascination of the Israeli-Arab conflict is that, like the Nigerian civil war or even, in some measure, the Belfast inferno, it is on a human scale and of a moral complexity that are normally only available to us in modern times in works of art like Shakespeare's history plays; so that probably there too an ironical stance will become more appealing to intellectual onlookers as the complexities become more insistently apparent. In contrast to the Camp evasions and the Godardian numbness, the higher irony has the advantage of being able to seem intellectually profound, not only through its associations with tragedy but in the epistemological questionings of a Hawthorne or a Melville or a Conrad. But, prestigious or not, the attitude seems to me a dangerous one. It is all too liable to degenerate into the havering one finds in the plays of that conscientious articulator of the British liberal conscience during the strife-torn pre-1914 years, John Galsworthy, in which there is always so much to be said for both sides that it becomes impossible to commit oneself to either – or to work out an alternative and superior course of action.[3] And involved in such a stance there is usually some dishonesty about the question of consequences.

As I said earlier, one of the liberal illusions is that one can always go home again if one chooses; and entailed in it is the feeling that no course of action, once embarked upon, is really irreversible and that nothing dreadful waits for one at the end of any road. In this respect there is very little difference between a movie like Zinneman's *A Man for All Seasons* and all those cartoons of cost-free heroism in which Jerry Mouse and Tweetie Pie and Droopy win, win always and effortlessly, because they are the right size or their hearts are in the right place. Part of the obnoxiousness of Zinneman's movie, in addition to Robert Bolt's vulgarization of the intellectual issues involved, was that nowhere in it was it indicated convincingly that this was indeed a time of, to use Thom Gunn's phrase, 'wheels, racks, and fires'. Hence the viewer was permitted a self-congratulatory identification with More the intellectual, without any sense of the appalling physical price that More faced paying as a result of his convictions, or any embarrassing self-questioning as to whether he himself would have been willing to pay it, or any related assessment of how much value he would be prepared to put on the life of the mind and on scrupulously-made mental distinctions. And a more sophisticated evasiveness about consequences seems to me discernible at times in the works of Conrad.

Not only are all the 'good' characters in *Nostromo* accorded the protection of a magic shield and spared from any violence in the course of the revolution. Even the torturing of Dr Monygham by Father Beron takes place off stage and is structurally unrelated to the main action; and the character who *is* tortured on stage by the forces of darkness is contemptible and his torturer a clown. Were the far from comic Guzman Bento or Fr Beron brought into the main action, the political victory of liberal democracy at the end of the novel would look more respectable than it does, the alternative being so horrible. And the dead weight of Decoud's final scepticism, which threatens to drag down with it all the ideals articulated in the course of the novel, would be much less persuasive if the result of the failure of those ideals were seen to be, as with the failures of intelligence in *King Lear*, not merely mediocrity but disaster. For that matter, Heyst's paralysis in *Victory* would have been left without any shreds of intellectual respectability had Conrad been able to sustain convincingly the asserted menace of the invading trio and give substance to Heyst's thought of Lena, after his prospective death at their hands, 'exposed helplessly to insult, outrage, degradation, and infinite misery of the body' (part IV, ch. 8). Far from being metaphysically profound, in fact, Conrad's scepticism, like Galsworthy's hesitancies and the irony of a politician like Balfour, seems to me to have been a product of the same kind of socio-political malaise, the increasing estrangement of thought from action, that resulted among other things in the enthusiasm with which so many people welcomed the outbreak of war in 1914. The scepticism is significantly absent from works like 'Typhoon' and 'The Shadow Line', in which the claims of the physical environment are ineluctable and must be met with responsible action in defence of others. And in *La peste*, similarly, Camus counters both the felt nihilism articulated in *L'Étranger* and the whole tradition of ironical scepticism by intensifying the physical exactions of the environment.

Once again, therefore, it is a great merit of some of the violences that I have been talking about in these pages that they make it harder to ignore certain facts, such as the intensity with which some convictions are held, and the implacability with which some people act on their beliefs, and the fact that in some conflicts both parties cannot be winners and that beyond a certain point one has to choose between them if one wishes to retain one's intellectual self-respect. In the Israeli-Arab conflict, for example, as in Shakespeare's major plays, every intellectual position either promotes or retards particular courses of action in an unusually clear way. One needs, of course, to be as aware as possible of the sentiments and sufferings on both sides, at least if one doesn't want to be the kind of applauder of violences who, in Orwell's words in 'Inside the Whale', 'is always somewhere else when the trigger is pulled'. But one still has to decide, sooner rather than later, which party one backs and agree that if violence is essential for its survival it must use violence. In other words, one has to come to judgment. And, in general, violence or the possibility of violence is a great sharpener of judgment.

There are, of course, a variety of *non*-violent ways in which a will to dominate or injure others can manifest itself. The goals of the calculating predatoriness in *Les liasions dangereuses*, for instance, may not be death or physical suffering, but the predatoriness is nonetheless atrocious on that account, and would remain so even if it did not bring about the deaths that it does. Scarcely less shocking at times are the cooler modes of total disrespect for another person's individuality that are displayed by figures like Gilbert Osmond in *The Portrait of a Lady* and Grandcourt in *Daniel Deronda*, and that flash out in some of the more memorable instances of actual reported rudeness – as when, for example, the leader of a delegation of Scottish professors visiting Victorian Oxford remarked cheerily to Benjamin Jowett, 'You mustn't think too hardly of us for our rough manners, Master,' and Jowett answered, 'We don't think about you at all.'[4] And in the novels of Jane Austen, even when rudenesses aren't involved, one is conscious all the time of the weightiness of language and the opportunities for wounding others in situations where etiquette makes it impossible for them to avoid unwelcome encounters. One is reminded by such works of how everyone's life style implicitly aggresses against everyone else's from which it sharply differs, in that it offers itself as normative and makes a challenge that has to be dealt with.[5]

It is in violent encounters, however, that one is required most obviously to reaffirm or reassess one's own values and to acknowledge the necessity of having as strong and clearly articulated a value-system, as sharply defined a self, as much alertness to others, and as firm a will as possible. There is of course a common desire to shirk or gloss over these obligations, particularly among people in the various bureaucratic systems – educational, governmental, commercial – who in some measure possess power over the lives of others and prefer that fact to be obscured from those whose lives they are affecting. And this kind of evasion has been facilitated by a particular manoeuvre with respect to the term 'violence'. I am speaking of the way in which politically respectable violence is not considered to be violence at all and the term is reserved for actions that are denied political significance or are felt to possess the wrong kind. As Albert Bienen writes in *Violence and Social Change*, 'There is a deep strain in British writing which sees insurgency as springing from man's inherent and compulsively irrational urge to violence and mischief' (p. 54), and it is not confined to Britain either. In this view of things, the military and the police, for example, are not violent organizations, and the 'problem' of violence is thought of as demanding what Bienen, in a slightly different connection, calls a 'therapeutic' approach or attitude (p. 38). So far as my own reading goes, the dominant concern of American psychologists and sociologists is to find ways of preventing people, without regard to their ideas, from engaging in any violences except those that suit the holders of power. But what has been increasingly made plain during the past few years, starting with the exposure of the fallacy of describing Vietnam as a 'police' action, is that the machinery of power is never neutral and that what violences frequently indicate is that one group has been making excessive claims to authority over another.

This process of revelation has involved making clear among other things, as Arendt pointed out, how the very notions of order and reasonableness could themselves be made part of the machinery of oppression, whether of the young being 'socialized' so as to fit compliantly into a particular economy, or Blacks, or women, or the lower orders generally. As Arendt observes, it is often, at bottom, not injustice but hypocrisy that provokes violence. And it is partly to the actual rules of the game that student 'confronters' have been trying to recall academics, and a greater honesty and accountability that they have been demanding. After all, there may not be as wide a gap as one would like to imagine between the affable liberal academic who says, 'I don't really like such-and-such myself either, you know, but I'm afraid you'll never be able to change the system,' and the 'decent' German involved unprotestingly in the bureaucracy of extermination. And implicit in the confrontations of the 1960s in general – educational, political, racial, sexual – was the effort to bring out that there is no such thing as a non-political position where organizations and one's attitude towards them is concerned.

But to adopt such a view – and it is itself a political one, of course – is not in the least to advocate what is often referred to as mindless violence. As I have tried to show, it is for the most part as much an error to think of violences as mindless as it is to attempt to gloss over the sanctified violences of society by referring to them as 'force'. As Freud observed in 1932,

> Thus we see that right is the might of a community. It is still violence, ready to be directed against any individual who resists it: it works by the same methods and follows the same purposes. The only real difference lies in the fact that what prevails is no longer the violence of an individual but that of a community.[6]

Blowing someone to bits is just as much violence whether the person doing it is getting rid of an unwanted relative, or is a member of a clandestine organization, or wears a government uniform. So is manhandling someone from a room, whether he be a middle-aged heckler at a Fascist meeting, or a student occupying a University official's office, or a boorish drunk at a party. So are some of the ways of subduing people in the name of a benevolent concern for their own good, such as forcing electro-shock therapy on them. To say all that, however, is not to attempt to blur distinctions. On the contrary, it is to insist on their ineluctability and on the necessity of making them precisely. *Pace* Auden, violence is not always and unequivocally bad. It depends on who is using it, and to whom, and why, and with what results. Which is another way of saying that all things come back ultimately to judgment and thought.

When I quoted Artaud earlier about the way in which the right kind of theatre 'causes the mask to fall, reveals the lie, the slackness, baseness, and hypocrisy of our world', I left the assertion incomplete. It ends: '. . . and in revealing to collectivities of men their dark power, their hidden force, it invites them to take, in the face of destiny, a superior and heroic attitude they would never have assumed without it' (p. 32). I believe that this is true of the right kinds of violent works. And what one again and again gets back to in such works is not body but mind. This is obvious enough with a number of the works that I mentioned in chapter 5: the *Odyssey* is a study in resourcefulness and diplomacy, Xenophon's *The March Up Country* is a study in practical intelligence and political leadership, *Sir Gawain and the Green Knight* is a study in self-mastery, and so on. But the same holds true even in less obvious areas, so that there is a kinship between such seemingly disparate works as, on the one hand, Grimm's fairy tales and the best thrillers, and, on the other, the Alice books and the novels of Jane Austen. In Grimm it is usually the courage, the alertness, the inventiveness of the hero or heroine that are being tested. In some of the best thrillers, such as *Rogue Male* or *Date with Darkness*, the challenges to the hero are at least as much mental as physical. In the Alice books, likewise, one is confronted with the steady strong impingement of other individualities on Alice herself, and even though no physical violences are actually inflicted on her, her situation is still continually one in which she must defend herself or be put down, and in which constant alertness is demanded – ask the question wrongly and get no answer; misinterpret an answer and find a door locked or one's body turning against one; lose one's head metaphorically and lose it literally. And as one passes from the Alice books – with their risks and traps, and astonishing rudenesses, and insistent claims of people to authority over the heroine – to the world of Jane Austen, one is reminded anew that a really worthwhile kind of polite culture is one that doesn't dull the mind and blur responses but heightens and sharpens awareness and makes for more effective conduct. Even where non-dramatic art is concerned, there is a major truth to Yeats' comment, apropos of a pair of landscapes, that 'neither painting could move us at all, if our thought did not rush out to the edges of our flesh, and it is so with all good art. . . .' The kinaesthetic fineness and toughness and consistency of organization in the work of Ben Jonson, and Walter Raleigh, and Thomas Wyatt, for example, is of a sort that would be as appropriate to the world of physical action as to the world of art.

To be prepared to endure violences is usually nobler than to wish to inflict them; and most of us, contemplating the heroism of a More or a Solzhenitsyn, can only feel profoundly thankful to live in societies in which we can do our thinking without serious physical risks. But the attitude in the following passage from a letter by Philip Sidney seems to me estimable nonetheless:

> Few words are best. My letters to my father have
> come to the eyes of some. Neither can I condemn
> any but you for it. If it be so you have played the
> very knave with me; and so I will make you know it
> if I have good proof of it. But that for so much as
> is past. For that is to come, I assure you before God,
> that if ever I know you do so much as read any letter
> I write to my father, without his commandment, or my
> consent, I will thrust my dagger into you. And trust
> to it, for I speak it in earnest. In the meantime,
> farewell.[7]

In this, as in a number of the instances of violence that I have pointed to in these pages, the focused intensity obviously comes from a powerful sense of what gives life dignity and of what boundaries cannot be crossed without an intolerable self-betrayal or betrayal of others; and it makes no essential difference, in that perception of things, whether the dagger is literal or metaphorical. Far from being mindless, violence is usually the cutting edge of ideas and ideologies. What counts above all is the clarity, integrity, and validity of one's thought, the completeness of one's commitment to one's own ideas, and a clear-sighted understanding of the ways in which, in the short or the long run, those ideas connect with the physical world, the world in which violences occur. And to the extent that thinking, especially the thinking of those in positions of power, ceases to have those virtues, to that extent we are increasingly going to have the kinds of violence that fail to achieve their ends or that achieve ignoble ones.[8]

NOTES TO THE TEXT

PREFACE, pp. ix–xii

1 A particularly challenging example of the formalist approach is Lawrence Alloway's *Violent America: the American Action Movie, 1945–1962* (N.Y., Museum of Modern Art, 1971).
2 'The Erotic and Censorship', *Oxford Review*, 9 (Michaelmas 1968), 21–39. Though it has been overtaken by events in one or two places, its arguments still seem to me essentially sound. See too in this connection Susan Sontag's brilliant 'The Pornographic Imagination', *Styles of Radical Will* (N.Y., Farrar, Straus & Giroux, 1969), pp. 35–73.

CHAPTER 1, 'INTRODUCTORY', pp. 1–13

1 Susan Sontag, 'Notes on "Camp"', *Against Interpretation: and Other Essays* (London, Eyre & Spottiswoode, 1967), p. 287.
2 Hannah Arendt, *On Violence* (N.Y., Harcourt, Brace & World, 1970), p. 8. Partly because of the relative absence of ethnic tensions, partly for other reasons that I shall glance at later, British thinking about violence has tended to be less simplistic than American in certain areas. It could presumably not have been said of Britain in 1966, for example, what Bruno Bettelheim said of the United States – 'Right now, the stories we teach . . . in class never contain any incidents of aggression. No child ever hits, becomes angry, or destroys things in an outburst. The worst they do is to tease or to pout. All of them live on Pleasant Street, in Friendly Town' – or what Albert Goldman said a couple of years later, apropos of the West Coast rock group The Doors: 'The important point about [their] anger is its calculated violation of a taboo. For in the overthrow of so many old prohibitions, there has grown up a new structure of forbidden things and denied emotions – and the first of these is anger.' (Bruno Bettelheim, 'Violence: a Neglected Mode of Behavior', in Shalom Endleman, ed., *Violence in the Streets* [Chicago, Quadrangle Books, 1968], p. 43; Albert Goldman, 'The Emergence of Rock', *This Magazine is about Schools*, II (Autumn, 1968), 85.) But D. W. Winnicott felt it necessary to assert in 1954 that 'The main idea behind this study of aggression is that if society is in danger, it is not because of man's aggressiveness but because of the

repression of personal aggression in individuals' (D. W. Winnicott, 'Aggression in Relation to Emotional Development', *Collected Papers: through Paediatrics to Psycho-Analysis* [London, Tavistock Publications, 1958], p. 204), and as the debate in the 1960s about aggression demonstrated, the subject of violence is still, on both sides of the Atlantic, a minefield of conflicting implications about the nature, needs, and potentialities of man as a social animal. See, for example, M. F. Ashley Montagu, ed., *Man and Aggression* (N.Y., Oxford University Press, 1968), Claire and W. M. S. Russell, *Violence, Monkeys and Men* (London, Macmillan, 1968), Edwin A. Megargee & Jack E. Hokanson, eds., *The Dynamics of Aggression: Individual, Group and International Analyses* (N.Y., Harper & Row, 1970), Irenäus Eibl-Eibesfeldt, *Love and Hate: the Natural History of Behavior Patterns*, trans. Geoffrey Strachan (N.Y., Holt, Rinehart & Winston, 1972), and Roger N. Johnson, *Aggression in Man and Animals* (Philadelphia, W. B. Saunders, 1972), as well, of course, as Robert Ardrey, *The Territorial Imperative* (N.Y., Athenaeum, 1970 [1966] and Konrad Lorenz, *On Aggression*, trans. Marjorie Kerr Wilson (N.Y., Bantam Books, 1967 [1966]).

3 Robert Warshow, 'Movie Chronicle: The Westerner', *The Immediate Experience*, ed. Sherry Abel (Garden City, N.Y., Doubleday Anchor Books, 1962), pp. 103–4. All references to Warshow are to this text.

4 G. Legman, *Love and Death: a Study in Censorship* (N.Y., Hacker Art Books, 1949); Fredric Wertham, *Seduction of the Innocent* (N.Y., Rinehart, 1954).

5 All quotations from Orwell are taken from *The Collected Essays, Journalism and Letters of George Orwell*, ed. Sonia Orwell and Ian Angus (4 vols., Harmondsworth, Middlesex, Penguin Books, 1970).

6 A selection from a small sub-group of the comics that Wertham attacked is provided in Ron Barlow and Bhob Stewart, eds., *Horror Comics of the 1950's* (Franklin Square, N.Y., Nostalgia Press, 1971). Warshow's 'Paul, the Horror Comics, and Dr. Wertham', *The Immediate Experience*, pp. 44–62, deserves to be read in conjunction with it.

7 On the violent pulps, see Tony Goodstone, ed., *The Pulps: Fifty Years of American Pop Culture* (N.Y., Chelsea House, 1970).

8 See, e.g., Thomas F. Berger's assertion that the Bond books were never best-sellers until Kennedy said they were among his favourite reading, and that they 'sold out after receiving [his] imprimatur'. 'Films', *Esquire* (June 1972), p. 61.

9 T. S. Eliot, 'Wilkie Collins and Dickens' (1927), *Selected Essays*, rev. and enl. ed. (London, Faber & Faber, 1934), p. 422.

10 *Time* (24 June 1965), p. 34.

11 Quoted years ago by James Agate, as I recall. His own translation, I seem to remember, was something like, 'I need to roll in the mud a bit.'

12 Hilde T. Himmelweit, A. N. Oppenheim, and Pamela Vince, *Television and the Child: an Empirical Study of the Effect of*

Television on the Young (London, Oxford University Press, 1965 [1958]).

13 Hans Toch, *Violent Men: an Inquiry into the Psychology of Violence* (Chicago, Aldine Publishing Co., 1969), p. 1.
14 Maurice Edgar Coindreau, introduction to André de Lorde, *Trois Pièces d'Epouvante* (N.Y., Henry Holt, 1934), p. vii.
15 Carlos Clarens, *An Illustrated History of the Horror Film* (N.Y., Capricorn Books, 1968), p. 155.
16 James Mayo, *Hammerhead* (London, Heinemann, 1964). In a a more recent book of Mayo's, a would-be strangler's eyes are sprung from their sockets by means of one of those corkscrews that releases compressed carbon-dioxide through a hollow spike.

CHAPTER 2, 'AMBIVALENCES', pp. 14–39

1 'Repertory', *Time* (3 January 1969), p. 51.
2 James Mills, 'The People Vs.', *Life* (30 August 1968), pp. 29–57. It has been reprinted, I believe, in Mills' *The Prosecutor* (N.Y., Farrar, Strauss, 1969).
3 Pamela Hansford Johnson, *On Iniquity: Some Personal Reflections Arising out of the Moors Murder Trial* (London, Macmillan, 1967), p. 66.
4 To speak of being violently raped may seem tautologous. However, John M. MacDonald's *Rape: Offenders and Their Victims* (Springfield, Ill., Charles C. Thomas, 1971) very usefully illuminates the range of events, including the range of participants, that the term 'rape' covers.
5 *A Woman of Berlin*, trans. James Stern (N.Y., Harcourt Brace, 1954).
6 See, e.g., Jean Paulhan's imagined question by Sade: 'About the woman you mistreat, are you quite sure that from abuse she does not derive some obscure and lascivious satisfaction?' 'The Marquis de Sade and His Accomplice', in Marquis de Sade, *The Complete Justine, Philosophy in the Bedroom and Other Writings*, comp. and trans. Richard Seaver and Austryn Wainhouse (N.Y., Grove Press, 1965), p. 20.
7 For an exceptionally pure specimen of the genre, in a chemical sense, see Oscar Millard, *A Missing Person* (N.Y., David McKay Co., Ives, Washburn, Inc., 1972). It comes complete with a quoted reference by Denis de Rougemont to 'the times when the nomad hordes suddenly appeared on the lands of the first settlers, pillaged, raped their women, taught them pleasure in the keenness of dread, and galloped back to their wasteland'. I will also mention what may well be the most powerful visual expression of the myth, namely a colour print by Utamaro in which a stiffly-robed young woman sits demurely on a river's grassy bank gazing pensively into the limpid water where, down below, a naked figure (herself?) is ecstatically being ravished by two demons.
8 While Apollinaire's statement that 'this man who appeared not to count for anything throughout the nineteenth century could well dominate the twentieth' (quoted by Raymond Jean,

'Sade et le surréalisme', in Centre Aixois d'Études et de Recherches sur le Dix-Huitième Siécle, *Le marquis de Sade* [Paris, Librairie Armand Colin, 1968], p. 243) is no doubt excessive, the works of Sade are indeed susceptible of being thought of as lying 'behind' a good many more recent ones; as being somehow more than merely another *oeuvre*; as being, almost, a natural phenomenon. Among the things that make them difficult to cope with in the normal way are: the sheer size of books like *La Nouvelle Justine* and *Juliette*; the plethora of matters touched on in them; the intermingling of ideas that have since become standard parts of modern thought and ones that are merely 'period'; the interweaving of arguments that are all on the side of liberty, equality and fraternity with ones that only make sense as parts of the self-justificatory systems of people profiting from radically inegalitarian structures; the historical problem of which of the presented social iniquities are pure fantasy and which ones were to be encountered in pre-Revolutionary Europe; and the critical problem created, apropos of the question of what Sade 'really' thinks, by the fact that all the narratives and speeches in *Juliette*, and a good many of those elsewhere, are in the technical sense, dramatic and not authorial.

9 What is probably the best American 'underground' erotic novel, the anonymous *The Devil's Brand* (or *The Devil's Advocate*) is urbane, amused, and un-sadistic.

10 Louis Perceau, *Bibliographie du roman érotique ou XIXᵉ siècle* (2 vols., Paris, Georges Fourdrinier, 1930).

11 'Sade', in Marquis de Sade, *Complete Justine*, pp. 50–1.

12 *Histoire d'O* may well be the only erotic novel that gives conscious masochism an intellectual content and makes it intellectually interesting. There is an almost unavoidable element of make-believe in conscious masochism, as Gillian Freeman reminds us in *The Undergrowth of Literature* (London, Nelson, 1968). Sadists do at times, very horribly, go the limit, sometimes by virtue of their official roles. Masochists, on the other hand, however much they may yearn with part of their minds to be utterly at someone else's mercy, are almost inescapably in the position of having to make sure that they really aren't in any serious danger.

13 Henri Alleg, *La question* (Paris, Les Éditions de Minuit, 1958); *La gangrène* (Paris, Les Éditions de Minuit, 1959); Simone de Beauvoir and Gisele Halimi, *Djamila Boupacha* (N.Y., Macmillan, 1962).

14 *Studies in Classic American Literature*, ch. 9.

15 On whom see Robert M. Coates, *The Outlaw Years: the History of the Land Pirates of the Natchez Trace* (N.Y., Macaulay, 1930).

16 Diana Trilling, 'Capote's *Crime and Punishment*', *Partisan Review*, xxxiii (Spring 1966), 252–9.

17 Cf. 'Obsessed as we were by these tortures, a week did not go by that we did not ask ourselves: "Suppose I were tortured, what would I do?" And this question alone carried us to the

very frontiers of ourselves and of the human.' Jean-Paul Sartre, *What is Literature?*, trans. Bernard Frechtman (London, Methuen, 1967), p. 162.

18 Donald Hamilton, *The Steel Mirror*, ch. 6.

19 In *The Third Theatre* (N.Y., Knopf, 1969), Robert Brustein symptomatically overpraises Kubrick's *Dr. Strangelove* ('it may well be the most courageous movie ever made') on the curious grounds that, among other things, 'Kubrick has managed to explode the right-wing position without making a single left-wing affirmation; the odor of the Thirties, which clung even to the best work of Chaplin, Welles, and Huston, has finally been disinfected here. Disinfected, in fact, is the stench of all ideological thinking' (p. 237).

20 J. Huizinga, *The Waning of the Middle Ages* (Garden City, N.Y., Doubleday Anchor Books, 1954), p. 151.

21 Remy de Gourmont, 'Women and Language' [1901], *Selected Writings*, trans. and ed. Glenn S. Burne (Ann Arbor, U. of Michigan Press, 1966), pp. 133–4.

22 Hannah Arendt, *The Origins of Totalitarianism*, 2nd enl. ed (Cleveland, World Publishing Co., 1958), p. 82.

23 See, e.g., 'There is no ruling class here, only a Darwinian struggle that divvies up Americans into winners and losers.' Paul D. Zimmerman, 'Movies' *Newsweek* (1 January 1973), p. 55. See also the memorable use of the term by George C. Scott in Rossen's, *The Hustler*.

24 Nathan Glazer, 'Blacks, Jews, and the Intellectuals', *Commentary* (April 1969), p. 36.

25 E. M. Forster, 'Three Anti-Nazi Broadcasts' [1940], *Two Cheers for Democracy* (London, Edward Arnold, 1951), p. 49.

26 Quoted in Dorothy Rabinowitz, 'Power in the Academy: a Reminiscence and a Parable', *Commentary* (June 1969), p. 48. The article is an admirable analysis of relationships between, on the one hand, authoritarianism, pseudo-professionalism, and intellectual corruption in American universities, and, on the other, violences in those institutions.

27 In *On Violence*, Arendt notes how the New Left's first reaction to what they had learned from their parent's generation about the totalitarian horrors of the 1930s and 1940s 'was a revulsion against every form of violence, an almost matter-of-course espousal of the politics of non-violence' (p. 14).

28 See for example Anatol Rapoport's comments on the new American military 'realists', especially: 'The Neo-Clausewitzians' view of man and society is typically a projection of the power-wielders' obsessions. They tend to obscure, dismiss, or ignore whatever role nurturing, cooperative, creative, or humane impulses may have played or may still play in human history.' Introd. to Carl von Clausewitz, *On War*, ed. Anatol Rapoport, trans. J. J. Graham (Harmondsworth, Middlesex, Penguin, 1968), p. 422.

29 Several movies in the early 1970s, such as Medford's *The Hunting Party* and Nelson's egregious *Soldier Blue* have involved the pitiless deployment of massive force against

powerless victims; and their appeal seems to me to have lain not in any oblique critical allusions to the Vietnam war but in their offering people the chance to indulge in feelings that they could not decently indulge in with respect to the war itself. (The direct treatment of violence stemming from the war in Compton's *Welcome Home, Soldier Boys* is quite another matter.) And if episodes like the beating-up in Mario Puzo's *The Godfather* or the torture scene in Frederick Forsyth's *The Day of the Jackal* are more disgusting than anything that Orwell attacked, it is because those violences are presented respectfully as demonstrations of the power of very powerful organizations.

CHAPTER 3, 'REVOLT', pp. 40–50

1 Arthur Miller, 'The Bored and the Violent', in Endleman, *Violence in the Streets*, pp. 270–9. Cf. Johnson, *On Iniquity*, p. 38: '"I did it for a joke." "It was a bit of a giggle." "*I was bored.*" The last is the most touted excuse of all, touted especially by hooligans who have wrecked an infant school, smashed every telephone booth in an area, where somebody without a telephone of his own might desperately need a doctor or an ambulance, beaten up a middle-aged man or woman for "kicks"'.

2 Norman Mailer, 'Talking of Violence' (as interviewed by W. J. Weatherby), in Endleman, *Violence in the Streets*, p. 88.

3 Paul Goodman, *Growing Up Absurd: Problems of Youth in the Organized Society* (N.Y., Vintage Books, 1960); Edgar Z. Friedenberg, *Coming of Age in America; Growth and Acquiescence* (N.Y., Vintage Books, 1965). Some of Goodman's findings would not have been entirely novel to British readers familiar with the approach stemming from F. R. Leavis and Denys Thompson's *Culture and Environment* (London, Chatto & Windus, 1933).

4 Arendt, *On Violence* (N.Y., Harcourt, Brace & World, 1970), pp. 65–6.

5 See, in this connection, Jean-Jacques Lebel's polemic on behalf of Happenings, 'Theory and Practice', in *New Writers IV: Plays and Happenings* (London, Calder & Boyars, 1967), pp. 13–45, especially statements like: 'All transmutation begins with a rape, with a reversal. . . . It is *avant-garde* art that . . . transfigures us and changes our conception of life. . . . The breaking of bonds is the very essence of poetry. . . . We no longer paint battles – we wage them. . . . The random element, the non-respect of taboos, the broadening of awareness – these constitute an indictment of the falsehoods of civilization and of the rules for living which it lays down everywhere. . . . On all sides, artistic action finds itself obliged to go beyond the pitiful limits of legality. . . . Authentic avant-garde art, contrasted with its civilization, is naturally revolutionary.' Lebel's argument, stemming as it does from Artaud and Surrealism, and including, as it does, such assertions as, 'Thus we dispute

the right of banal outbreaks of violence to be called Happenings' (p. 28) is more complex than these statements suggest. But the sequence that I have strung together constitutes what can almost be called the official *avant-garde* argument, and it is obviously highly susceptible of vulgarization, particularly in America. Significantly, the shortened version of Lebel's article that appeared in the *Tulane Drama Review*, 13 (Fall 1968) 89–105, was titled 'On the Necessity of Violation'.

6 See in this connection Laurence Kitchin, *Drama in the Sixties* (London, Faber & Faber, 1966), pp. 21–2.

7 The admirable discussion ensuing after Stanley S. Collier's lucid 'Surréalisme et théâtrologie', in Ferdinand Alquié, ed., *Entretiens sur le surréalisme* (Paris, La Haye Mouton, 1968), pp. 220–45, is of considerable interest in this connection.

8 There has been a noticeable increase in the killing of animals in movies, such as Godard's *Weekend*, which probably started it, Schmidt's *The End of August at the Hotel Ozone*, Guerra's *The Gods and the Dead*, Wise's *The Andromeda Strain*, and Kotcheff's *Outback*. The first three, at least, are serious works; and obviously vastly more suffering has been involved in all those innumerable action movies, such as Aldrich's disgusting *Ulzana's Raid*, in which horses at full gallop are deliberately brought crashing down. But the trend still deserves to be viewed with suspicion.

9 All quotations from Artaud are taken from *The Theater and Its Double*, trans. Mary Caroline Richards (N.Y., Grove Press, 1958).

10 See Georges Arnaud et Jacques Vergès, *Pour Djamila Bouhired* (Paris, Les Éditions de Minuit, 1961), pp. 50–1.

11 A case can also be made for the referentiality of a work like Richard Schechner's seemingly antithetical theatre-of-cruelty *Dionysus in 69*, but to do so, if in fact the case needs making, would take me too far from the main line of my argument.

12 André Breton, *Manifestoes of Surrealism*, trans. Richard Seaver and Helen K. Lane (Ann Arbor, U. of Michigan Press, 1969), p. 213.

13 Significantly the notion of 'violation' is entirely absent from the theoretical writings of Artaud's most distinguished successor, Jerzy Grotowski, assembled in his *Towards a Poor Theatre*, ed. Eugenio Barba (N.Y., Simon & Schuster, 1970).

14 Diana Trilling, 'On the Steps of Low Library: Liberalism and the Revolution of the Young', *Commentary* (November 1968), p. 43.

15 Ezra Pound, *ABC of Reading* (London, George Routledge, 1934), p. 13.

CHAPTER 4, 'VICTIMS', pp. 51–82

1 The term 'Ruthless Rhymes' is taken from Harry Graham's *Ruthless Rhymes for Heartless Homes; and More Ruthless Rhymes for Heartless Homes* (N.Y., Dover, 1961). I do not

know who the author of the quoted example was. It goes back at least to the 1930s.

2 The two statements come respectively from Sade, *The 120 Days of Sodom and Other Writings*, comp. and trans. Austryn Wainwright and Richard Seaver (N.Y., Grove Press, 1966), p. 639, and 'Slaughter of the Hutus', *Newsweek* (26 June 1972), p. 40.

3 Where humour is concerned, everyone has doubtless had the experience at some age of laughing himself or herself sick over the opening pages of a novel – Evelyn Waugh's *Vile Bodies*, say – and then finding the effect diminishing sharply as he or she proceeds. The same thing, if my own experience is anything to go by, happens where the erotic stimulation of reading Sade is concerned.

4 'It was a lion, fastened to a cross by its four limbs like a criminal. Its huge muzzle hung down on its chest, and its fore-legs, half hidden under the abundance of its mane, were spread wide like the wings of a bird. Its ribs stood out separately under its taut skin; its hind legs, nailed together, were drawn up a little; and black blood trickling through its hair had collected in stalactites at the end of its tail, which hung straight down the length of the cross' (ch. 2).

5 The failure of sympathy in the second instance does not invalidate the flow of it in the first, of course, and one can feel profoundly grateful for the eminently practical and commonsensical activities of the animal welfare organizations at work in North Africa as described in Monica Hutchings and Mavis Carver's *Man's Dominion: Our Violation of the Animal World* (London, Rupert Hart-Davis, 1970), ch. 10.

6 See, e.g., some of the photographs in Frederick A. Barber, ed., *The Horror of It: Camera Records of War's Gruesome Glories* (N.Y., Brewer, Warren & Putnam, 1932), or three of the four photographs of Arabs mutilated by the F.L.N. in Jacques Massu, *La Vraie Bataille d'Alger* (Paris, Plon, 1972) – photographs none the less horrible for being reproduced in such a context.

7 E.g., 'Unless you have lived through it yourself, you could never understand. All the photographs and documents in the world, even seeing the piles of corpses with your own eyes, would never explain what it was like. . . . For one thing they were nowhere as bad as you think – and at the same time, they were infinitely worse than anything you could ever imagine. Even I, after more than a year there, cannot talk about it without feeling as if I were making it all up. Either that, or telling a dream that someone else had dreamed.' Former concentration-camp inmate, quoted by Raymond Guthrie in introd. to David Rousset, *The Other Kingdom*, trans. Raymond Guthrie (N.Y., Reynal & Hitchcock, 1947).

8 Introd. to *The Oxford Book of Modern Verse* (Oxford, Clarendon Press, 1936), p. xxxiv.

9 Eugen Kogon, *The Theory and Practice of Hell: the German Concentration Camps and the System behind them*, trans.

Heinz Norden (London, Secker & Warburg, 1950); David
Rousset, *L'Univers concentrationnaire* (Paris, Éditions du
Parvois, 1946) [*The Other Kingdom*], Viktor E. Frankl, *Man's
Search for Meaning* (Boston, Beacon Press, 1962); Primo Levi,
If This is a Man, trans. Stuart Woolf (London, Orion Press,
1959); Tadeusz Borowski, *This Way for the Gas, Ladies and
Gentlemen; and Other Stories*, trans. Barbara Vedder (London,
Jonathan Cape, 1967).

10 Part of the enduring appeal of the Western is that the horses
are really being ridden over those salt-flats or through those
rivers by those stars; and a greatly intensified form of this
appeal is to be found in Boorman's *Deliverance*, a work which
in some ways answers uncommonly closely to the account of
successful violences given in this chapter. In one respect,
however, its hyperrealism works against it. One is so conscious
of the skill of the actors as they simultaneously steer their
canoes through the rapids and impersonate their respective
characters that when one is faced with the two 'corpses',
one is primarily aware of the actors' ability to hold their
breaths and not blink. Friedkin's admirably physical *The
French Connection* did not suffer in this way.

11 On British attitudes to Franju (who seems to me the most
distinguished living French director, next to Renoir) and to
revolt in cinema generally, see Raymond Durgnat's *Franju*
(London, Studio Vista, 1967), which belongs with Ado Kyrou's
Le surréalisme au cinéma, édition mise à jour (Paris, Le
Terrain Vague, 1963) as not only the best work on its
subject, but one of the most stimulating books on cinema.

12 Louis-Ferdinand Céline, *Death on the Installment Plan*, trans.
Ralph Mannheim (N.Y., New Directions, 1966), p. 29.

13 It seems to be pretty much a commonplace by now among
investigators that, where children are concerned, identification
with violent people is more likely to come when they are
'good' than when they are 'bad'. See, e.g., Himmelweit and
others, *Television and the Child*; André Glucksmann, *Violence
on the Screen: a Report on Research into the Effects on Young
People of Scenes of Violence in Films and Television*, trans.
Susan Bennett (London, British Film Institute Education
Department, 1971); and BBC Audience Research Department,
*Violence on Television: Programme Content and Viewer
Perception* (London, British Broadcasting Corporation, 1972).

14 Guy Chapman, ed., *Vain Glory; a Miscellany of the Great
War, 1914–1918* (London, Cassell, 1968 [1937]).

15 In André de Lorde, *Théâtre de la peur* (Paris, Librairie
Théâtrale, 1924). In this connection, see also André de Lorde
and Henri Bauche, *Les drames célèbres du Grand Guignol*
(Paris, Librairie Stock, 1924).

16 *The Iliad of Homer*, trans. Richmond Lattimore (Chicago,
U. of Chicago Press, 1961), p. 341.

17 See also, where the implements of death or injury are
concerned, the sensed alienness of the Green Knight's axe when

Gawain first hears it being sharpened ('What! it wharred and whette, as water at a mulne [mill]') and the way in which during the fight in the woods in Richardson's *Tom Jones* a sword (the picturesque ornament of innumerable costume movies) suddenly becomes a murderously pointed piece of metal giving a fearsome advantage to the man holding it, and the way, too, in which Jack Palance's gunning-down of Elisha Cook, Jr, in Stevens' *Shane* suddenly brings into focus the dreadful potentials of that picturesquely noisy metal contraption known as a 'revolver'.

18 See also, in this connection, Orwell's 'A Hanging'.

19 Jan Luiken, *Schouwtooneel der Martelaren (Théâtre des Martyrs)*, (n.p., M. Schagen, 1738). The series is described, misleadingly, in Huysman's *À rebours*.

20 Both of the quoted passages come from Hannah Arendt, *Eichmann in Jerusalem; a Report on the Banality of Evil* (N.Y., Viking Press, 1963), pp. 83, 173.

21 Bettelheim also points to the paradox that small injuries, such as slaps and abuse, were often felt and resented more than large ones, such as beatings; and he suggests that the reason may have been that the former were too poignantly related to normal life outside the camps.

22 *A Sign for Cain; an Exploration of Human Violence* (N.Y., Macmillan, 1966), p. 187.

23 The revolt of servants is a peculiarly emotion-charged subject, whether in the atrocious actuality of the Papin sisters or in Losey's non-violent but very cruel *The Servant*. And the rage produced at times by the merest hint of 'insolence' in the serving class, where there is one, obviously derives from the feared collapse of a very profitable set of rules. If the master (or mistress) refrains from behaving insolently towards the servant, this is essentially not an acknowledgment of the individuality and rights of the latter, but a manifestation of the spirit of *noblesse oblige*. If, on the other hand, the servant refrains from insolence towards the master, this is no more than the master's due, a recognition of his innate inviolability as a member of the superior class.

CHAPTER 5, 'VIOLATORS', pp. 83–108

1 One reason why the paintings of Francis Bacon are mostly not as disturbing as they offer to be is probably that the anguishes and disasters in them appear not to have been caused but merely to have happened, in contrast to those in Goya's work or even in some of Edward Kienholz's, where agents are sensed even when not shown. An obvious exception is 'Three Studies for a Crucifixion'.

2 As E. S. Turner's *All Heaven in a Rage* (London, Michael Joseph, 1964) suggests, the history of the humanitarian movement may have been complicated at times by class conflicts, or conflicts between different subcultures. But an indifference towards the sufferings of animals on the part of

supposedly educated and enlightened people seems to me always cause for alarm, sometimes grave alarm. The moral climate of nineteenth-century vivisection, for example, was not only loathsome in itself because of the frequent atrociousness of the sufferings and the callousness of those responsible. (On which see, for example, Frances Power Cobbe, *The Modern Rack: Papers on Vivisection* [London, Swan Sonnenschein, 1893] and Albert Leffingwell's *The Vivisection Controversy; Essays and Criticisms* [London, The London and Provincial Anti-Vivisection Society, 1908], both of which deserve to be reprinted.) It was also, if not the first, then certainly the most dramatic manifestation thitherto of the claim of researchers, in the name of science, to be beyond the reach of any control, inspection, or judgment whatsoever except what it suited them to acknowledge. As John Vyvyan points out in *The Dark Face of Science* (London, Michael Joseph, 1971), it led quite directly to the horrors of the Nazi medical experiments, experiments conducted for the most part by thoroughly respectable and well-intentioned scientists, with the complicity of a good many others. (On whom see Alexander Mitscherlich and Fred Mielke's *Doctors of Infamy: the Story of the Nazi Medical Crimes*, trans. Heinz Norden [N.Y., Henry Schuman, 1949] and *The Death Doctors*, trans. James Cleugh [London, Elek, 1962].) And of course the tradition still goes on. If the animal experimenters in behavioural psychology, for example, were offered *carte blanche* in prisons and mental hospitals to extend their researches in sensory deprivation, pain-elicited aggression, and the like, can anyone doubt that there would be applicants to take advantage of it?

3 See, e.g., Colin Watson's statement that by the end of the 1930s, 'detective fiction was accounting for one quarter of all new novels published in the English language' (*Snobbery with Violence: Crime Stories and Their Audience* [London, Eyre & Spottiswoode, 1971], p. 96). On the atmosphere of a good deal of pre-war crime fiction, see also Julian Symons, *Bloody Murder: from the Detective Story to the Crime Novel; a History* (London, Faber & Faber, 1972), Erik Routley, *The Puritan Pleasures of the Detective Story: from Sherlock Holmes to Van der Valk* (London, Victor Gollancz, 1972), and Richard Usborne, *Clubland Heroes* (London, Constable, 1953).

4 Though there was undoubtedly exaggeration for propaganda purposes, it is clear from the *Report of the Committee on Alleged German Outrages* (2 vols., London, HMSO, 1915) that a good many atrocities were indeed committed in Belgium, not casually but as a matter of policy.

5 Lewis Yablonsky, *The Violent Gang* (Harmondsworth, Middlesex, Penguin, 1967).

6 Robert Benayoun, 'Zaroff, ou les prosperités du vice', *Présence du cinéma*, numéro special 6/7 (Décembre 1960), pp. 9–10.
  It is essential to add that the true Sadist thinks of constraint not as an instrument of injustice or oppression, but as a test of character. . . . It is impossible for him, for example,

except by a disastrous error, to subjugate free spirits like himself; he would become their victim in his turn. . . .

We are at the opposite extreme here from the insensitive executioner or the degenerate criminal; our hero is usually a highly cultured and insolently courteous man, who displays very often a fine sense of humour, thinks of crime as a work of art and of love ('Everything on which Sade sets his seal is love,' says Gilbert Lely), and faithfully abides by the rules of his own game, even to the point of becoming the victim of it himself.

The same odd – and inaccurate – emphasis on 'fairness' appears in George de Coulteray's *Le sadisme au cinéma* (Paris, Le Terrain Vague, n.d.). See, for example, his assertion, apropos of the claim that 'The [Sadean] chateau has absolutely nothing in common, either in principle or in practice, with the concentration camp,' that, 'Paradoxical though it may be, the "victims" are not subjected to any constraints. . . . The odds at the outset are scrupulously even. At every point the strong will have to give proof of their strength, and the weak will be so only because they are willing to submit to them' (pp. 133–4).

7 On whom see especially Georges Bataille, *Le procès de Gilles de Rais* (Paris, Jean-Jacques Pauvert, 1965) and Valentine Penrose, *The Bloody Countess*, trans. Alexander Trocchi (London, Calder & Boyars, 1957).

8 On the sisters, see, e.g., Stephen Barlay, *Bondage: the Slave Traffic in Women Today* (N.Y., Funk & Wagnalls, 1968), pp. 112–115, and *Newsweek* (2 November 1964), p. 60. On the princess, see Rowland W. Black, *Histoires et crimes de la Gestapo parisienne* (Brusselles, Exclusivités de vente ASA, 1945', pp. 105–13.

9 Of Romano, Raymond Rudorff observes in *Monsters: Studies in Ferocity* (London, Neville Spearman, 1968) that 'he appeared as a phenomenon, as the human incarnation of the fiercest and most destructive forces of nature, as a kind of human hurricane tearing through his time, wrecking everything in his path. He is the greatest, most awe-inspiring figure in all the Italian chronicles of the thirteenth century' (p. 68).

10 Simone de Beauvoir, 'Must We Burn Sade?', in Sade, *The 120 Days of Sodom*, p. 8.

11 Pierre Favre, *Sade utopiste: sexualité, pouvoir et état dans le roman 'Aline et Valcour'* (Paris, Presses Universitaires de France, 1967).

12 Guy Molino, 'Sade devant la beauté', in Centre Aixois d'Études et de Recherches sur la Dix-Huitième Siécles, *Le marquis de Sade*, p. 166, a book that seems a model of responsible academic discussion of Sade.

13 F. M. Dostoevsky, *Memoirs from the House of the Dead*, trans. Jessie Coulson (London, Oxford University Press, 1956), pp. 216–17.

14 Jorge Semprun, *The Long Voyage*, trans. Richard Seaver (Toronto, McClelland & Stewart, 1964), p. 71.

15 Helmut Krausnick and others, *Anatomy of the SS State*, trans. Richard Barry, Marian Jackson, Dorothy Long (London, Collins, 1968), p. xv. The book itself, especially the two long chapters by Martin Bucheim, seems an admirable example of what Krausnick desiderates.

16 Kevin Brownlow, *How It Happened Here*, Cinema One (London, Secker & Warburg, 1968), p. 43.

17 Quoted by Alastair Hamilton, *The Appeal of Fascism: a Study of Intellectuals and Fascism* (London, Anthony Blond, 1971), p. 253.

18 Kogon, *The Theory and Practice of Hell*, pp. 207–8, 210.

19 Friedrich Nietzsche, *The Birth of Tragedy and The Genealogy of Morals*, trans. Francis Golffing (Garden City, N.Y., Doubleday Anchor Books, 1956), p. 174.

20 Richard Roud, *Jean-Luc Godard*, Cinema One, 2nd rev. edn (London, Thames & Hudson, 1970), p. 40. There is what sounds like a somewhat analogous documentary short by Ziarnik, *L'Homme de la Gestapo, Schmidt*, in which an individual Gestapo man is recreated for us with the aid of letters, snapshots, and so on.

21 See, e.g., David Rousset, *Les jours de notre mort* (Paris, Éditions de Pavois, 1947).

22 See, for example, the to my mind somewhat equivocal tone of Heinz Höhne's massive *The Order of the Death's Head: the Story of Hitler's SS*, trans. Richard Barry (London, Secker & Warburg, 1969).

23 One of the oddest things about *Hitler's Table Talk, 1941–1944*, trans. Norman Cameron and R. H. Stevens (London, Weidenfeld & Nicholson, 1953) is how *American* its tone is in some ways – not gangster America, but the America of the slightly old-style self-made millionaire, the at times inspired inventor, the corner-cutter and streamliner, the disregarder of precedent, protocol and habit, the contemptuous anti-intellectual and self-proclaimed ordinary man whose contempt nevertheless comes in part from a sense of understanding better than intellectuals and 'experts' what the inner springs of history and culture really are, the amateur of grandiose architecture and conspiratorial occultist theories, the endower of crackpot foundations, the defender of the nation against mongrelization and communism.

24 Geoffrey Gorer, *The Life and Ideas of the Marquis de Sade*, enl. and rev. edn (London, Peter Owen, 1953), p. 115.

25 Albert Camus, *The Rebel*, trans. Anthony Bower (London, Hamish Hamilton, 1953), p. 43.

26 Quoted by Raymond Jean, 'Sade et le surréalisme', in Centre Aixois, *Le marquis de Sade*, p. 247.

27 See Hamilton, *The Appeal of Fascism*, p. 186.

28 They are well presented in Pierre Favre's *Sade utopiste*. Basically Sade seems to me to have been attempting two different things in his works. One was to argue in what were essentially still Enlightenment terms that a good many punitive attitudes, especially those concerning sex, were not

only unjust but unwarranted, since a more liberal approach would better achieve the results that they were supposed to achieve. The other was to articulate a vision of an ideal anti-Enlightenment and anti-Christian world corresponding to his own intensest imaginings, and to reassure himself that its dynamics and ethics were as coherent and workable as those of the systems that condemned him to imprisonment and ignominy. Since he tried to do both things rationalistically in terms of a near-contemporary Europe, this made for unresolvable contradictions and involved him in contending with equal passion that in practice people like himself were socially harmless and that in theory they should be permitted to realize their most destructive desires.

29 André Breton, ed., *Anthologie de l'humour noir* (Paris, Jean-Jacques Pauvert, 1966), pp. 39–40.

30 Ernst Nolte, *Three Faces of Fascism: Action Française, Italian Fascism, National Socialism*, trans. Leila Vennewitz (N.Y., Holt, Rinehart & Winston, 1966), p. 289.

31 I have been unable to recall where I found this quotation.

32 Quoted by Hamilton, *The Appeal of Fascism*, p. 272.

33 Pol Vandromme, *Pierre Drieu la Rochelle*, Classiques du XX¹ᵉ siècle (Paris, Éditions Universitaires, 1958), p. 112.

34 See Hamilton, *The Appeal of Fascism, passim*. Cf. also Arendt's reference to 'the terrifying roster of distinguished men whom totalitarianism can count among its sympathizers, fellow-travellers, and inscribed party members', and her immediately following observation that, 'This attraction for the elite is as important a clue to the understanding of totalitarian movements as their more obvious connection with the mob.' *The Origins of Totalitarianism*, 2nd enl. edn (Cleveland and N.Y., World Publishing Co., 1958), p. 326.

35 Quoted by Hamilton, p. 216.

36 Ernst Jünger, *The Storm of Steel: from the Diary of a German Storm Troop Officer on the Western Front*, trans. Basil Creighton (London, Chatto & Windus, 1929).

37 R. H. Tawney, *The Attack; and Other Papers* (London, George Allen & Unwin, 1953), pp. 21–8.

38 *The Storm of Steel*, p. xii.

39 Pierre-Joseph Proudhon, *Selected Writings*, ed. Stewart Edwards, trans. Elizabeth Fraser (London, Macmillan, 1970), p. 207.

40 William James, 'The Moral Equivalent of War', *The Writings of William James; a Comprehensive Edition*, ed. John J. McDermott (N.Y., Random House, 1967), pp. 661, 666.

41 The first, which has been reproduced more than once, can be found in Jean Roman, *Paris fin de siècle*, trans. James Emmons, Golden Griffin Books (N.Y., Essential Encyclopedia Arts, Inc., 1960). The other was reproduced in *Paris-Match*, I think in the summer of 1966.

42 Much of the strength of the *mafiosi* in America, in actuality as well as in art, plainly comes from the fact that they are the only group outside of the South who are sustained by a lucid

and long-established code by virtue of which the perpetrators of violences are behaving perfectly normally and honourably.
43 J. Glenn Gray, *The Warriors: Reflections on Men in Battle* (N.Y., Harper & Row, 1967).

CHAPTER 6, 'THOUGHT', pp. 109–32

1 A. Alvarez, *The Savage God: a Study of Suicide* (London, Weidenfeld & Nicolson, 1971), p. 32.
2 *The Portable Nietzsche*, p. 530.
3 The nastiness of the manhandling in Hitchcock's *The Trouble with Harry* and *Frenzy* seems to me entirely different – the result simply of a callous schoolboyish refusal to think of the manhandled object as having ever been alive to begin with. In Jonathan Latimer's ostentatiously hard-boiled 1930s thriller *The Lady in the Morgue*, the bodies figuring prominently in it have at least *been* alive, though the graveyard humour is still bothersome. I have not seen Bacon's gangster comedy from the 1930s, *A Slight Case of Murder*, but from what I have read about it the manhandled corpse in it figures as something that almost *is* still alive – the near-equivalent of someone who has inconveniently passed out from alcohol or drugs and has to be kept out of sight.
4 'The dead lay face down in the mud, or emerged from shell holes, peacefully, their hands on the edges of the holes, their heads resting on their arms. The rats came and sniffed them. They hopped from one to another. They chose the young ones first, those without beards on their cheeks. They sniffed their cheeks, then they settled down and began to eat the flesh between the nose and the mouth, then the edges of the lips, then the unripe apples of the cheeks. From time to time they passed their paws through their whiskers to clean them. As for the eyes, they got them out with little taps of their paws and licked out the eye-sockets; then they bit into the eyes, as if they were little eggs, and chewed them gently, their heads on one side, sucking out the juice' (Part II, 3rd section).
5 Baudelaire, 'Les sept vieillards'. 'In vain my reason wanted to take the helm;/ The tempest, sporting, sent its efforts astray,/ And my soul danced, danced, like an old lighter/ Without masts, on a monstrous, shoreless sea.'
6 Nietzsche, *Beyond Good and Evil*, trans. Walter Kaufmann (N.Y., Vintage Books, 1966), p. 89.
7 Cf., "The truth we are reluctant to face is that there is no depravity and no cruelty that is beyond the ingenuity of quite ordinary men who are otherwise amiable and even conventional.' *Manchester Guardian*, quoted by Wertham, *A Sign for Cain*, p. 367.
8 E. M. Forster, 'What I Believe', *Two Cheers for Democracy* (London, Edward Arnold, 1951), p. 82.
9 As in, for example, Robert Allerton and Tony Parker's very interesting *The Courage of His Convictions* (London, Hutchinson, 1962), the reminiscences of an intelligent,

articulate, apparently incorrigible, and, when necessary, violent professional criminal.

10 If Sade in contrast continues to remain disturbing, it is not because of the violences themselves or because of what they show or are presumed to show about human nature and human potentials. Except for the brothel parts of *Les cent vingt jours*, one is almost always conscious of Sade *talking* his violences, for one purpose or another, as part of an argument – *his* violences, rather than violences emanating from consciousnesses that are alien from his, and that could have been encountered in actual cities or countrysides. And *Juliette*, his best book, disturbs for much the same reason that *Mein Kampf* or *Understanding Media* do. It disturbs because of the aggressiveness of the assertions, the continuous monstrous overemphases, and the general intellectual unscrupulousness, and because the mixture of half-truths, truths, and sheer falsehoods requires of the reader a constant alertness which rapidly becomes fatiguing.

11 'It was a male with black tufts on his head. His two large twisted horns stretched out like the branches of an oak. He had rested the horns on the backs of the sheep on either side of him so that his heavy head was being carried along; his head with its horns was borne along on the flood of animals like the stump of an oak tree on the Durance in flood. There was clotted blood on his teeth and inside his lips.

'The bend in the road pushed him towards the side. He tried to hold up his head by himself, but it dragged him down towards the ground; he struggled with his forelegs, then he knelt down. His head lay there on the ground like a dead thing. He struggled with his hind legs, then he fell in the dust like a pile of wool that had just been cut. He spread his thighs with little painful jerks; the whole area between his thighs was a morass of blood, with flies and bees moving around in it and two red eggs which were only fastened to the groin by a nerve as thick as a piece of string' (Part I, 1st section).

12 This kind of cruelty on the part of the author can of course be found also in non-violent works, such as Benjamin Constant's *Adolphe*, Choderlos de Laclos' *Les liaisons dangereuses*, and a poem like Baudelaire's 'Le Jeu'.

13 In George Grosz, *Interregnum* (portfolio) (N.Y., Black Sun Press, 1936), p. 51.

14 Michel Caen, '"Scialytique . . . Caméra . . . Moteur!"', *Midi-Minuit Fantastique*, numéro 10–11 (Hiver 1964–5), p. 70.

15 The question of whether or not filmed violences are 'cathartic' is obviously partly a critical one, and discussion of it seems to have been bedevilled by an unwillingness to get involved in critical questions. The term 'catharsis', where tragedy is concerned, points to a real psychological phenomenon: one leaves the theatre after certain performances feeling emptied out and in some measure relaxed, in a beneficial way. At the same time, not all works that offer themselves as tragedies are capable of producing that feeling, and neither are all

productions even of distinguished tragedies: one can leave the
theatre after a bad production of *Othello* feeling tense and
irritable. The same variousness obtains with respect to
bloodshed and gruesomeness in movies. Watching certain horror
movies, among them Bava's *Sei Donne per l'Assassino (Blood
and Black Lace)* and some of the Hammer ones that used to
upset British reviewers so much, can in my experience be
genuinely cathartic. And they are cathartic because the
shocking parts provide climaxes to certain movements or
phases in them and permit certain actions to reach their
logical conclusions and certain formal anticipations to be fully
satisfied, just as they are satisfied in non-bloody works, such as
slapstick comedies. So too with the bloodbaths in Westerns
like Leone's *For a Few Dollars More*, Corbucci's *Django*, and
at a higher level, Peckinpah's *The Wild Bunch*. The production
of catharsis is not in itself a mark of distinction in a work or
spectacle, of course, and no doubt it would be a better world
if nobody enjoyed bloodbaths, or read thrillers, or watched
wrestling, and so on. Moreover, a number of bloody movies,
like a good deal of what goes on in the fight industry no doubt,
are morally disgusting. (I should perhaps confess here that I
could not bring myself to see Russell's *The Devils* at all.) But
that is not a sufficient reason for preventing consenting adults
from seeing them, provided that laws against cruelty itself
aren't violated. And if what is at issue is the state of mind in
which people come out from movie theatres, I can only suggest
that they will sometimes be less tense and aggressive after
watching gruesome movies than when they went in.

16 *The Portable Nietzsche*, p. 518.
17 In John Ford's *'Tis Pity she's a Whore*, for instance, which
   Artaud admired so much, one is obviously back to a kind of
   childhood level of conceptualization in which, as in *Ubu Roi*,
   desire translates itself into action with virtually no thinking at
   all, let alone debating or pondering.
18 In this connection the reiterated testimonials to the *non-
   monstrousness* of S.S. men can hardly be over-emphasized,
   supporting as they do Arendt's assertion that: 'The trouble
   with Eichmann was precisely that so many were like him, and
   that the many were neither perverted nor sadistic, that they
   were, and still are, terribly and terrifyingly normal' (*Eichmann
   in Jerusalem*, p. 253). E.g.: 'I knew hardly a single SS man
   who could not say that he saved someone's life. There were
   few sadists. No more than five or ten per cent were criminals
   by nature. The others were perfectly normal men. . .' (Dr Ella
   Lingens-Reiner, Auschwitz prisoner, quoted by Höhne, *The
   Order of the Death's Head*, p. 382); 'Many of them were
   quite dangerous, some were cruel, but only a small minority
   were actually perverted, stupid, bloodthirsty or homicidal'
   (Bettelheim, *The Informed Heart*, p. 224); 'Many concentration
   camp survivors report that it was only the earliest generation
   of SA guards that tortured prisoners for pleasure. The SS
   guards who followed them tended rather to be "businesslike"'

(David Schoenbaum, *Hitler's Social Revolution: Class and Status in Nazi Germany, 1933–1939* [Garden City, N.Y., Doubleday Anchor Books, 1966], p. 287). One of the more arresting things in Kogon's *Theory and Practice of Hell* is the quiet opening statement that 'Late in the fall of 1937, in Frankfurt, I had occasion for an extended discussion with a leading SS man from Vogelsang Castle [one of the S.S. elite centre] – a discussion that continued over several afternoons . . . [and] was very frank on both sides. . . . The SS officer was by no means stupid, indeed he had a superior intellect, for all that he was a thoroughgoing fanatic' (p. 15).

19 Significantly, however, the number of treatments of the Crucifixion in art that are kinaesthetically painful to contemplate, such as Gerard David's painting of the nailing to the cross, Grünewald's *Crucifixion*, and Rogier van der Weyden's *Pietà*, seems to be small. For the most part, at least in post-Gothic art, the event is converted into an almost games-playing, sado-masochistic display of near-nudity. And the early history of Christianity has been comfortably smoothed over by all the jokes about lions and Christians, and made erotically titillating by every arena movie so far. To lose sight of the actual arena horrors is to lose sight too of the demonic courage and compulsions of that remarkable faith.

20 It presumably derived from the apologia in Colonel Roger Trinquier's *La guerre moderne* (Paris, La Table Ronde, 1961), an apologia reiterated in Massu's own *La vraie bataille d'Alger*. The appeal of such a position should not be lightly dismissed, either. A good many readers who were in their teens during the Second World War must have wondered, if they were honest, how they themselves would act in a situation in which the only way in which some horror or disaster could be averted would be by compelling a Nazi prisoner to speak.

21 Bertrand Russell, *Power: a New Social Analysis* (N.Y., Norton, 1938), p. 83.

22 See *Les torturés d'El Harrach* (Paris, Les Éditions de Minuit, 1966). It is natural enough to feel when reading such a book (including the preface to it by Henri Alleg) that the systematic use of torture by a government that purports to be of the Left is one of the clearest signals that it is in fact moving away from the Left. And one of the most economical ways of differentiating between the Left and Right might seem to be to say that the use of torture is not only not incompatible with the principles of the latter but is almost bound to be a concommitant of them in one area or another. However, some of the observations by Pierre Vidal-Naquet in his *La torture dans la République; essai d'histoire et de politique contemporaines (1954–1962)* (Paris, Les Éditions de Minuit, 1972) deserve to be kept in mind here, such as, 'All dissent, whatever its nature, can push the modern state, however liberal it may be, to the use of torture' (p. 14), or the following: 'Every society which feels itself threatened by dissent . . . can perfectly easily, today or tomorrow, tolerate

a sporadic or systematic use of torture. . . . It is not only a certain conception of social conservatism which can lead the state to become a torturing state. It is also a certain conception of social revolution. . . . It would be reassuring – but false – to identify torture and conservatism. . . . Whoever has reflected in the slightest on the origins of Stalinism knows that it isn't so. . . . One could perhaps propose the following axiom: every apocalyptic conception of revolution – i.e., every conception . . . which assumes that a supremely bad state has abruptly been succeeded by, or will be succeeded by, a supremely good one . . . – , every conception built on this pattern is favourable by its very nature to the emergence of a torturing state . . .' (pp. 175–7).

23 See, e.g., Thomas S. Szasz, *The Manufacture of Madness; a Comparative Study of the Inquisition and the Mental Health Movement* (N.Y., Harper & Row, 1970).

24 See, e.g., the article ascribed to Colonel Trinquier and R. P. Delarue, 'Entre deux maux choisir le moindre', in Pierre Vidal-Naquet, ed., *La raison d'état; textes publiés par le comité Maurice Audin* (Paris, Les Editions de Minuit, 1962), pp. 112–22.

25 What makes the heretic so alarming to the orthodox is that his ability to pass through orthodoxy and come out the other side arouses the suspicion that he may have seen something that they have missed, and understood their system better than they have. In this connection it is interesting how completely the Japanese atrocities during the Second World War seem to have been forgotten, except, presumably, by those who were victims of them. The reason, I presume, is not merely the extraordinary changes in Japanese society since 1945. It is also the fact that, unlike the Nazi ones, they issued out of a *Weltanschauung* so alien that there could be no question of our feeling tempted to assent to any aspect of it.

26 Gerald Reitlinger, *The SS, Alibi of a Nation: 1922–1945*, 2nd rev. impr. (London, Heinemann, 1957), p. 451.

CHAPTER 7, 'RESPONSIBILITIES', pp. 133–51

1 Quoted in E. H. Carr, *The Romantic Exiles; a Nineteenth-Century Portrait Gallery* (Boston, Beacon Press, 1961 [1933]), p. 336, and A. Alvarez, *The Savage God: a Study of Suicide* (London, Weidenfeld & Nicolson, 1971), p. 41.

Johnson's accusation that, 'Not having found a major cause, they proceed to invest great emotional energy in minor ones; and of the minor ones, verbal emancipation takes a high place' (*On Iniquity*, p. 84), is no doubt true of a number of the opponents of censorship. But it seems to me susceptible of being turned back upon a good many of the proponents of it. And Morse Peckham, in *Art and Pornography; an Experiment in Explanation* (N.Y., Basic Books, 1969) in fact provides an ingenious argument to the effect that it is precisely because the subject, in terms of the larger structures of society, is

relatively trivial, that people are likely to go on trying to
censor sexual works: that is to say, the censorship game
provides reassurance that society is being properly 'policed',
while distracting attention from more serious social problems.
In any case, where violence is concerned, it seems fairly clear
that the attempt to 'protect' society from the display of the
more extreme violences is at bottom almost inescapably an
attempt to protect authority from disquieting challenges to it.
The most blatant example of this is the BBC's treatment of
Watkins' *The War Game*. But of course there have been other
examples.

Huston's documentary on mentally disturbed veterans, *Let
There be Light* (1945), for instance, was suppressed by the
U.S. authorities who commissioned it. Chelle's *Le départ des
forçats* (1930), a clandestine filming of the departure of
convicts for the French overseas penal settlements, and Hayer's
Exécution capitale (1930), a clandestine filming of a double
guillotining in a French prison, appear to have remained
virtually invisible. (Kyrou describes all three films briefly in
Le surréalisme au cinéma, p. 140.) Coulteray speaks of 'an
American documentary, never shown since just after the
Liberation because judged too atrocious for nice people,
[which] showed a G.I. opening the door of an oven and pulling
out the twisted and half-consumed corpse of a "sub-human".
Another shot displayed a corpse that had been burned by a
flame-thrower and transformed into a fragile and horrible
statue of cinders' (*Le sadisme au cinéma*, p. 52.) And where
the subtler censorship of financing and distribution is
concerned – a censorship that obviously gains strength from
the threat of actual censorship on the one hand and the
squeamishness of some reviewers on the other – one has such
disgraceful phenomena as the virtual suppression of Brownlow
and Mollo's *It Happened Here*, the fact that neither of them has
been able to make a film since, the fact that Watkins has had
to go outside England in order to continue filming at all, the
thwarting of so many of Franju's projects, and the long silence
of Buñuel between *La Hurdes* (1932) and *Los Olvidados*
(1950). As Kyrou observes, 'Society doesn't like to be
displayed naked. Documentaries annoy it even more than
fiction films; honest reporting is an axe hung over its head'
(p. 139). So at times is honest fiction.

It is noteworthy, moreover, that the kinds of movies that I
have been speaking of here are not open to Stephen Collier's
objection that 'The melancholy fate of "pure" theatre is to be
taken over by the bourgeoisie. The bourgeoisie always makes
a new play its own property.' (Alquié, *Entretiens sur le
Surréalisme*, p. 231.) (*The Brig*, incidentally, appears to have
escaped this fate. According to Laurence Kitchin in *Drama
in the Sixties: Form and Interpretation* [London, Faber &
Faber, 1966, p. 70], 'it did not draw the public, not even
the sizeable minority public that goes to the theatre for kicks'.)
The right kinds of documentaries on, for example, such horrors

as animal factories and the conditions of animals in American research laboratories as described by Vyvyan (*Dark Face of Science*, ch. 17) would challenge commercial and bureaucratic systems *because* they upset the viewer. An intelligent film on the latter subject would presumably also involve reflections upon the interrelations between the revealed callousness and cruelty, the mechanistic approach to the animals, and the fact that some of the explorations into nerve-gases, bacteriological warfare, and the like, are functions neither of so-called defence needs, nor of a desire to increase 'knowledge', but simply of the fact that scientists like to keep busy and advance themselves professionally and that they have a handy supply of living creatures to keep themselves busy with. But can anyone imagine that such a film would ever be permitted to be made, let alone distributed?

2 Pierre Vidal-Naquet, *Torture: Cancer of Democracy; France and Algeria, 1954–62*, trans. Richard Barry (Harmondsworth, Middlesex, Penguin, 1963), p. 147.

3 Quoted by Rudorff, *Monsters*, p. 158.

4 Quoted by Vidal-Naquet, *Torture: Cancer of Democracy*, pp. 175–7.

5 On some of the fundamental workings of that mind, see especially Bertrand de Jouvenel's brilliant *Power; the Natural History of its Growth*, 2nd rev. edn, trans. J. F. Huntington (London, Hutchinson, 1947).

6 It is a general truth, I suspect, that as long as someone whose position is under attack knows that there is a major element in it that his attacker has not taken into account, he will feel safe however much evidence and however many siege-engines of logic are brought up against him.

7 A sizeable area of British Literary–intellectual life since the 1920s could probably be illuminated by a careful comparison of the two men, a comparison taking into account their native abilities, their relationships to ideas, and their approaches to cultural history, especially British history.

8 Coulteray, *Le sadisme au cinéma*, p. 156.

9 Christopher Lasch, 'Getting Out of Power', *Commentary* (November 1965), p. 116.

10 Cf. Kyrou, apropos of Strand's *Heart of Spain*, on 'a sequence which belongs among the most revolutionary in the whole of cinema, because it places the spectator in front of his responsibilities and compels him to take sides – hence to revolt' (p. 140).

11 Gabriel Vialle, 'À propos de Georges Franju', *Image et son*, special issue on Franju (March 1966), p. 43.

12 W. H. Auden, 'The Bound and the Free', *Scrutiny*, IV (September 1935), 201.

13 See too William A. Westley's *Violence and the Police: a Sociological Study of Law, Custom and Morality* (Cambridge, Mass., The MIT Press, 1970).

14 Novels like MacDonald's *The Only Girl in the Game*, McPartland's *The Kingdom of Johnny Cool*, and John Reese's

The Looters provide a healthy corrective to Mario Puzo's sentimentalities in *The Godfather*.

15 See, e.g., Hunter S. Thompson, *Hell's Angels: a Strange and Terrible Saga* (N.Y., Random House, 1967), and Frank Reynolds, *Free-Wheelin' Frank; Secretary of the Angels*, as told to Michael McClure (N.Y., Grove Press, 1967).

16 'On Authority', in Karl Marx and Friedrich Engels, *Selected Works* (2 vols., Moscow, Foreign Languages Publishing House, 1951; pub. in Great Britain by Lawrence and Wishart), I, 577–8. Quoted by James Joll, *The Anarchists* (London, Eyre & Spottiswoode, 1964), p. 110.

17 I have discussed this aspect of *The Tempest* in '*The Tempest* Revisted', *Critical Review*, 11 (1968), 60–78.

18 On American violences, see especially Henry Davis Graham and Ted Robert Gurr, eds., *The History of Violence in America: Historical and Comparative Perspectives; a Report Submitted to the National Commission on the Causes and Prevention of Violences* (N.Y., Frederick A. Praeger, 1969), and Richard Hofstadter and Michael Wallace, eds., *American Violence; a Documentary History* (N.Y., Alfred A. Knopf, 1970).

19 'Doing without Consciousness', *Times Literary Supplement* (12 May 1972), p. 534.

20 See, for example, Ralph K. Andrist, *The Long Death: the Last Days of the Plains Indians* (N.Y., Macmillan, 1964).

21 As Paulhan points out in the afterword to *Histoire d'O*, Bartolomé de las Casas' *Brevissima Relacion de la Destruycion de las Indias* (*The Spanish Colonie*, March of America Facsimile Series, no. 8 [Ann Arbor, University Microfilms, Inc., 1966] makes shocking reading in its retailing of atrocities in Mexico. E. D. Morel's discussion of the activities in King Leopold's Congo, *Red Rubber: the Story of the Rubber Slave Trade flourishing on the Congo in the Year of Grace 1906* (N.Y., Negro Universities Press, 1969 [1906]) is much more infuriating, however, because of the odious hypocrisy and unconscionable lying that accompanied the atrocities there.

22 Cf. Arendt, 'The author of the imperialist legend is Rudyard Kipling, its topic is the British Empire, its result the imperialist character (imperialism was the only school of character in modern politics)' (*Origins*, pp. 208–9).

23 Two classic examples are Robert Penn Warren's *All the King's Men* and Hammett's *The Glass Key*, with their bifurcation between the socially injurious man of practical power and the more civilized ironical observer, in a seductive relationship that at bottom can be only corrupting for the latter. This dualism goes back through *The Great Gatsby* (which is heavily indebted to Conrad's *Heart of Darkness*) to at least Hawthorne's *The Blithedale Romance*.

24 The only American espionage novelist of comparable merit is Hamilton, and it is probably significant that almost all his novels are set on the North American continent. There are also few significant American movies to set beside Losey's admirable

exploration of the use of 'necessary' force by administrators in *We Are the Damned*.

25 W. B. Yeats, of course, had been in an Imperial situation from the start.

26 Despite its insufferably 'revolutionary' and mannered style, Jonah Raskin's *The Mythology of Empire: Rudyard Kipling, Joseph Conrad, E. M. Forster, D. H. Lawrence, and Joyce Cary* (N.Y., Random House, 1971) is of considerable interest in this connection.

CHAPTER 8, 'CONCLUDING', pp. 152–62

1 *The Classical Tradition* (London, Oxford University Press, 1927).

2 That it is missing from the vulgarly partisan *Aeneid* is partly a result of Virgil's manifest ignorance of what extreme violence feels like. Unable to project kinaesthetically into the fighting consciousnesses of those involved, and hence to feel deeply the moral complexities of battle, it is all too easy for him to heap unreal violence upon unreal violence in an another-Latin-bites-the-dust spirit. It deserves pointing out in this connection that Edmund Spenser, whose treatment of violence in *The Faerie Queene* is similarly questionable, was a wholehearted partisan of the most ruthless of the Elizabethan administrators who tried to terrorize the Irish 'natives' into submission.

3 'There's really quite a bit to be said for the striking miners, you know. But then on the other hand there's a lot to be said for the mine-owners too, of course. And really, who is to say who's *really* right? And both sides are going to lose, you know. In fact we're all going to lose. Oh dear, oh dear, it's all so tragic. Such a waste! Why can't people behave *better* towards each other?' (A parody, but not, I fear, a gross one.) A lack of ultimate commitment is especially easy where drama is concerned; the responsibility for the various utterances can be shifted off onto the characters, and if the characters themselves aren't acting with a full and intelligent commitment, well, that, of course is simply part of *their* natures, and not of the dramatist's.

4 E. F. Benson, *As We Were* (London, Longmans, Green, 1930).

5 See for example the disproportionate indignation that can be induced by a friend's complacent refusal to try a dish or drink that one especially relishes oneself.

6 'Why War?' (exchange with Albert Einstein, September 1932), in *The Standard Edition of the Complete Psychological Writings of Sigmund Freud*, trans. and ed. James Strachey, in collaboration with Anna Freud (London, Hogarth Press and the Institute of Psycho-Analysis, 1964), xxii, 205.

7 Quoted by Bonamy Dobrée, *Modern Prose Style* (Oxford, Clarendon Press, 1934), pp. 215–16.

8 Uneven as it was, *A Clockwork Orange* touched only too convincingly on this relationship. It can be advanced as a

general principle that to the extent that candour, intellectual integrity, and a willingness to assume responsibility for one's actions have ceased to inform the workings of a bureaucratic structure, to that extent those involved have forfeited the right to be morally indignant about the violences of others. They have forfeited the right to speak on behalf of reason.

INDEX

187